Activities for the Differentiated Classroom

Gayle H. Gregory • Carolyn Chapman

For information:

Corwin Press
A SAGE Publications Company
2455 Teller Road
Thousand Oaks, California 91320
CorwinPress.com

SAGE, Ltd.
1 Oliver's Yard
55 City Road
London EC1Y 1SP
United Kingdom

SAGE India Pvt. Ltd.
B 1/I 1 Mohan Cooperative
Industrial Area
Mathura Road, New Delhi
India 110 044

SAGE Asia-Pacific Pvt. Ltd.
33 Pekin Street #02-01
Far East Square
Singapore 048763

Printed in the United States of America.

ISBN 978-1-4129-5339-9

This book is printed on acid-free paper.

08 09 10 11 12 10 9 8 7 6 5 4 3 2 1

Executive Editor: Kathleen Hex
Managing Developmental Editor: Christine Hood
Editorial Assistant: Anne O'Dell
Developmental Writer: Barbara Allman
Developmental Editor: Carolea Williams
Proofreader: Bette Darwin
Art Director: Anthony D. Paular
Cover Designer: Monique Hahn
Interior Production Artist: Scott Van Atta

Activities *for the* Differentiated Classroom

GRADE **3**

TABLE OF CONTENTS

Connections to Standards

This chart shows the national academic standards that are covered in each chapter.

MATHEMATICS	Standards are covered on pages
Numbers and Operations—Understand numbers, ways of representing numbers, relationships among numbers, and number systems.	13
Numbers and Operations—Understand meanings of operations and how they relate to one another.	16
Numbers and Operations—Compute fluently, and make reasonable estimates.	9
Algebra—Understand patterns, relations, and functions.	18
Geometry—Use visualization, spatial reasoning, and geometric modeling to solve problems.	21
Measurement—Understand measurable attributes of objects and the units, systems, and processes of measurement.	15
Data Analysis and Probability—Formulate questions that can be addressed with data, and collect, organize, and display relevant data to answer them.	23
Data Analysis and Probability—Select and use appropriate statistical methods to analyze data.	11
Problem Solving—Apply and adapt a variety of appropriate strategies to solve problems.	27

SCIENCE	Standards are covered on pages
Science as Inquiry—Ability to conduct scientific inquiry.	42
Physical Science—Understand light, heat, electricity, and magnetism.	49
Life Science—Understand characteristics of organisms.	39
Earth and Space Science—Identify objects in the sky.	45
Earth and Space Science—Understand changes in the earth and sky.	38
Science in Personal and Social Perspectives—Understand changes in environments.	32
History and Nature of Science—Understand science as a human endeavor.	33

SOCIAL STUDIES	Standards are covered on pages
Understand the ways human beings view themselves in and over time.	58, 61
Understand the interactions among people, places, and environments.	50, 53
Understand how people create and change structures of power, authority, and governance.	59
Understand global connections and interdependence.	65
Understand the ideals, principles, and practices of citizenship in a democratic republic.	55, 63

LANGUAGE ARTS	Standards are covered on pages
Read a wide range of literature from many periods in many genres to build an understanding of the many dimensions (e.g., philosophical, ethical, aesthetic) of human experience.	67
Apply a wide range of strategies to comprehend, interpret, evaluate, and appreciate texts. Draw on prior experience, interactions with other readers and writers, knowledge of word meaning and of other texts, word identification strategies, and understanding of textual features (e.g., sound-letter correspondence, sentence structure, context, graphics).	69, 71, 74, 76, 78
Adjust the use of spoken, written, and visual language (e.g., conventions, style, vocabulary) to communicate effectively with a variety of audiences and for different purposes.	82
Apply knowledge of language structure, language conventions (e.g., spelling and punctuation), media techniques, figurative language, and genre to create, critique, and discuss print and nonprint texts.	81
Use spoken, written, and visual language to accomplish a purpose (e.g., for learning, enjoyment, persuasion, and the exchange of information).	79

Introduction

As a teacher who has adopted the differentiated philosophy, you design instruction to embrace the diversity of the unique students in your classroom and strategically select tools to build a classroom where all students can succeed. This requires careful planning and a very large toolkit! You must make decisions about what strategies and activities best meet the needs of the students in your classroom at that time. It is not a "one size fits all" approach.

When planning for differentiated instruction, include the steps described below. Refer to the planning model in *Differentiated Instructional Strategies: One Size Doesn't Fit All, Second Edition* (Gregory & Chapman, 2007) for more detailed information.

1. Establish standards, essential questions, and expectations for the lesson or unit.

2. Identify content, including facts, vocabulary, and essential skills.

3. Activate prior knowledge. Pre-assess students' levels of readiness for the learning and collect data on students' interests and attitudes about the topic.

4. Determine what students need to learn and how they will learn it. Plan various activities that complement the learning styles and readiness levels of all students in this particular class. Locate appropriate resources or materials for all levels of readiness.

5. Apply the strategies and adjust to meet students' varied needs.

6. Decide how you will assess students' knowledge. Consider providing choices for students to demonstrate what they know.

Differentiation does not mean always tiering every lesson for three levels of complexity or challenge. It *does* mean finding interesting, engaging, and appropriate ways to help students learn new concepts and skills. The practical activities in this book are designed to support your differentiated lesson plans. They are not prepackaged units, but rather activities you can incorporate into your plan for meeting the unique needs of the students in your classroom right now. Use these activities as they fit into differentiated lessons or units you are planning. They might be used for total group lessons, to reinforce learning with individuals or small groups, to focus attention, to provide additional rehearsal opportunities, or to assess knowledge. Your differentiated toolkit should be brimming with engaging learning opportunities. Take out those tools and start building success for all your students!

Put It into Practice

Differentiation is a Philosophy

For years teachers planned "the lesson" and taught it to all students, knowing that some will get it and some will not. Faced with NCLB and armed with brain research, we now know that this method of lesson planning will not reach the needs of all students. Every student learns differently. In order to leave no child behind, we must teach differently.

Differentiation is a philosophy that enables teachers to plan strategically in order to reach the needs of the diverse learners in the classroom and to help them meet the standards. Supporters of differentiation as a philosophy believe:

- All students have areas of strength.

- All students have areas that need to be strengthened.

- Each student's brain is as unique as a fingerprint.

- It is never too late to learn.

- When beginning a new topic, students bring their prior knowledge base and experience to the new learning.

- Emotions, feelings, and attitudes affect learning.

- All students can learn.

- Students learn in different ways at different times.

The Differentiated Classroom

A differentiated classroom is one in which the teacher responds to the unique needs of the students in that room, at that time. Differentiated instruction provides a variety of options to successfully reach targeted standards. It meets learners where they are and offers challenging, appropriate options for them to achieve success.

Differentiating Content By differentiating content the standards are met while the needs of the particular students being taught are considered. The teacher strategically selects the information to teach and the best resources with which to teach it using different genres, leveling materials, using a variety of instructional materials, and providing choice.

Differentiating Assessment Tools Most teachers already differentiate assessment during and after the learning. However, it is equally important to assess what knowledge or interests students bring to the learning formally or informally.

Assessing student knowledge prior to the learning experience helps the teacher find out:

- What standards, objectives, concepts, skills the students already understand

- What further instruction and opportunities for mastery are needed

- What areas of interests and feelings will influence the topic under study

- How to establish flexible groups—total, alone, partner, small group

Differentiating Performance Tasks In a differentiated classroom, the teacher provides various opportunities and choices for the students to show what they've learned. Students use their strengths to show what they know through a reflection activity, a portfolio, or an authentic task.

Differentiating Instructional Strategies When teachers vary instructional strategies and activities, more students learn content and meet standards. By targeting diverse intelligences and learning styles, teachers can develop learning activities that help students work in their areas of strength as well as areas that still need strengthening.

Some of these instructional strategies include:

- Graphic organizers

- Cubing

- Role-playing

- Centers

- Choice boards

- Adjustable assignments

- Projects

- Academic contracts

When planning, teachers in the differentiated classroom focus on the standards, but also adjust and redesign the learning activities, tailoring them to the needs of the unique learners in each classroom. Teachers also consider how the brain operates and strive to use research-based, best practices to maximize student learning. Through differentiation we give students the opportunity to learn to their full potential. A differentiated classroom engages students and facilitates learning so all learners can succeed!

CHAPTER 1

Mathematics

Grab the Lion

Standard
Numbers and Operations—Compute fluently, and make reasonable estimates.

Objective
Students will practice addition and subtraction facts with numbers from 0–18 to increase fluency.

Materials
Grab the Lion Cards reproducible
cardstock

Play this game as a whole group with students paired up to play against each other. The object is to snatch a lion card by knowing addition and subtraction facts and moving quickly! Games encourage students to activate their brains in a fun and engaging way. This game provides novelty, challenge, and feedback.

1. Copy the **Grab the Lion Cards reproducible (page 10)** onto cardstock. Cut out the cards on the solid lines. Then fold each card on the dotted line so there is an upright lion on each side of the card.

2. Divide the class into student pairs. Give each pair a folded lion card to place between them on a desk. Have players stand on opposite sides of the desk within reach of the lion card.

3. Say an addition or subtraction sentence aloud, such as: *5 + 11 = 16*. Students must decide if the statement is true or false. If the statement is true, each student tries to be the first in his or her pair to snatch the lion card off the desk. The student who grabs the lion first gets a point. Invite students to keep track of their points on scratch paper.

4. If the addition or subtraction statement is false, neither player should touch the lion card. If a player touches the lion card after hearing a false statement, he or she must give one of his or her points to the other player. The player who reaches 12 points first is the winner.

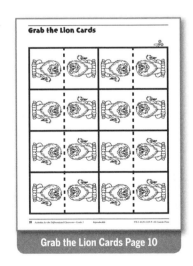

Grab the Lion Cards Page 10

Grab the Lion Cards

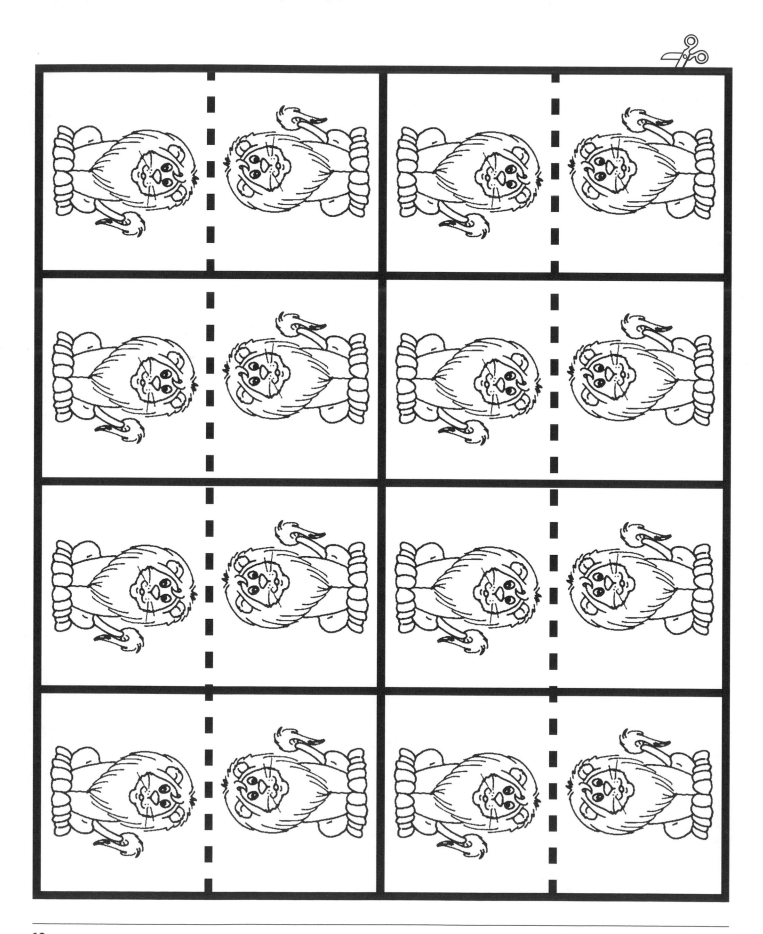

Home on the Range

Standard
Data Analysis and Probability—Select and use appropriate statistical methods to analyze data.

Objective
Students will find the range in a given set of data.

Materials
Home on the Range Number Cards reproducible
cardstock

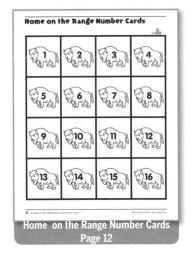

Stimulate students' brain power with an activity that challenges them to earn points by reaching a goal. This game is played independently. Students with logical/mathematical or intrapersonal learning styles can work at their own pace.

1. Reproduce the **Home on the Range Number Cards reproducible (page 12)** on cardstock. Give each student a copy of the cards to cut apart. Have students mix up their cards before placing them facedown in a pile.

2. Invite students to draw the top seven cards from the top of their card stack and place them face-up on the desk in numerical order.

3. Tell students that the difference between the highest and lowest number in their card set is called the *range*. To find the range, students must subtract the lowest number from the highest number. The range is the number of points they earn for this card set.

4. Have students keep track of their points on scratch paper. Then have players return the cards to the stack, shuffle the cards, and draw seven new cards. They will find the range, record it as their point value, and shuffle the cards again. Set a point value for students to reach. Once the goal is reached, the game is over.

Home on the Range Number Cards Page 12

Ideas for More Differentiation
Adapt this game to appeal to bodily/kinesthetic learners by creating teams of seven with one set of number cards. Team members each draw a card and line up in numerical order. They then determine their range. Have teams keep track of their scores on the board. The first team to reach 50 points wins.

Home on the Range Number Cards

  978-1-4129-5339-9 • © *Corwin Press*

Secret Code

Standard
Numbers and Operations—Understand numbers, ways of representing numbers, relationships among numbers, and number systems.

Strategies
Focus activity

Rehearsal

Objective
Students will show place value to the thousandths place.

Materials
Secret Code reproducible

Students with strong spatial skills enjoy learning when it involves visualizing and decoding. In this activity, spatial learners can practice place-value concepts by decoding digits to form numbers.

1. Give each student a copy of the **Secret Code reproducible (page 14)**. Invite students to identify each symbol in the Decoder and tell what place value it represents.

2. On the board, write the number *4,692* using symbols from the Decoder. Draw four stars, six triangles, nine boxes, and two dots. Ask students to write the number the secret code represents, and have a volunteer write it on the board.

3. Invite students to decode the secret numbers on their Secret Code reproducible. (Answers: 1. 1,242; 2. 4,131; 3. 263; 4. 3,504; 5. 5,024) Remind students that the symbols on their worksheet are not in place-value order.

4. Invite students to create their own secret number codes in the box at the bottom of the page. Have partners exchange papers to decode each other's numbers!

Secret Code Page 14

Ideas for More Differentiation
Interpersonal learners will enjoy working together to invent a code. Provide a number of self-stick dots in various colors. Have students work in small groups to invent a secret code using the colored dots and record their codes on a chart. For example, students might use green dots for thousands, blue dots for hundreds, red dots for tens, and yellow dots for ones. Invite students to make two or three numbers using their dot code.

Secret Code

Directions: Use the Decoder to discover the secret numbers.

Decoder	
Star ✱	= thousands place
Triangle ▲	= hundreds place
Box ■	= tens place
Dot ●	= ones place

Can you decode these numbers?

1. ▲▲ ✱ ●● ■■■■■   _____

2. ● ■■■ ▲ ✱✱✱✱   _____

3. ■■■■■■ ●●● ▲▲   _____

4. ●●●● ✱✱✱ ▲▲▲▲▲   _____

5. ✱✱✱✱ ●●●● ■■   _____

Make some secret number codes for a partner to decode.

_____

Measure This and Measure That

Standard
Measurement—Understand measurable attributes of objects and the units, systems, and processes of measurement.

Strategy
Mnemonic device

Objective
Students will use rhyme to recall units of weight in standard and metric units.

Teach a mnemonic device that will help students recall which units of measurement to apply when estimating weights. The rhyme will help them remember approximate weights for an ounce, a pound, a gram, and a kilogram.

Measure This and Measure That
Measure this and measure that,
Now put on your thinking hat.
Keep this thought inside your head:
One ounce is a slice of bread.

Measure this and measure that,
Now put on your thinking hat.
Keep this thought inside your head:
One pound is a loaf of bread.

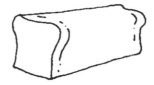

Measure this and measure that,
Now put on your thinking hat.
Keep this thought, don't let it slip:
One gram is a paperclip.

Measure this and measure that,
Now put on your thinking hat.
You can tell your good friend Sam.
His math book is a kilogram.

Ideas for More Differentiation
Copy the rhyme onto chart paper. Write the units of measure in a color different from the rest of the text. To aid visual/spatial learners, use cutout pictures or simple drawings to illustrate the items mentioned in the rhyme.

Dice and Beans

Standard

Numbers and Operations—Understand meanings of operations and how they relate to one another.

Objective

Students will demonstrate knowledge of addition, subtraction, multiplication, and division facts.

Materials

Dice and Beans Game reproducible

dice

dried beans

This hands-on math game engages students in a tactile experience that challenges them to earn points while reinforcing basic math skills.

Dice and Beans Game Board Page 17

1. Give each student a copy of the **Dice and Beans Game reproducible (page 17)** and a handful of dried beans. Students may play this game with a partner or in a small group of three or four players. Give each pair or group two dice. The object of the game is to cover the entire number grid with beans. Players earn a point for each number covered.

2. Instruct players to cover number *11* with a bean and place the remaining beans on the pot at the bottom of the grid. The first player rolls the dice and tries to add, subtract, multiply, or divide the numbers to get a number that touches 11 on the number grid. For example, if a player rolls two fives on the dice, he or she could multiply the numbers to get 25, which touches number 11 on the number grid. The player then places a bean on 25 and earns one point.

3. The next player rolls the dice and tries to make a number that touches either 11 or 25. If a player cannot add, subtract, multiply, or divide to make a number that touches a number already covered by a bean, the player must pass.

4. If a player rolls the dice and can add, subtract, multiply, or divide to get a number that touches two numbers already covered by a bean on the number grid, the player earns two points. The game continues until all the numbers on the grid have been covered by beans. At the end of the game, have players tally their points to determine the winner.

Dice and Beans Game

Directions: Roll two dice. Add, subtract, multiply, or divide the two numbers. If your answer is next to any number already covered by a bean on the grid, cover it with a bean.

Scoring:

Answer touches one number on the grid = 1 point

Answer touches two numbers on the grid = 2 points

3	10	24	18	8
36	15	5	11	4
30	1	25	7	16
12	20	6	2	9

Highways and Byways

Strategies
Build a model

Multiple intelligences

Standard
Algebra—Understand patterns, relations, and functions.

Objective
Students will make models of multiplication equations that multiply a number by three, and record the equations.

Materials
Highways and Byways reproducible
craft sticks
buttons

Using concrete objects to build a model helps build students' logical/mathematical skills. In this activity, students make arrays to represent products of three.

1. Introduce the activity by telling students they will make a map of highways and byways using craft sticks. Direct them to place three craft sticks vertically on the desk in front of them. You may wish to demonstrate this on an overhead projector. The sticks should be parallel and rest about one inch apart. Explain that these are called *highways*.

2. Have students place two craft sticks across the highways. These will be called *byways*. The two sticks should stretch across all three highways at right angles. Intersections are where the highways and byways cross.

3. Ask if anyone knows what is needed at each intersection (signal light). Have students place a button to represent a signal light at each intersection. Ask: *How many signal lights were needed?* (six)

4. Give each student a copy of the **Highways and Byways reproducible (page 20)**. Show students how to record their work. Have them write the number of highways (*three*), the number of byways (*two*), the number of signal lights (*six*), and then the equation to describe their model (*3 x 2 = 6*).

5. Give students directions to use different numbers of byways (0, 1, 3, 4, 5) to complete the chart. Help students discover a pattern, and ask them to predict the number of signal lights each time the number of byways changes.

6. Direct students to make their own map of sticks and draw it in the space at the bottom of their worksheet. Challenge them to invent a word problem about their map. For example: *There are three highways crossed by three byways. One byway closed during rush hour because the signal lights weren't working. How many signal lights weren't working?* (three) Invite students to trade papers with a partner so they can solve each other's problem.

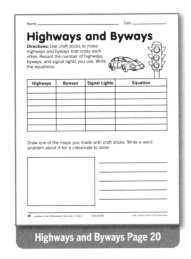

Highways and Byways Page 20

Ideas for More Differentiation

Students with strong logical/mathematical intelligence will enjoy making their own highways-and-byways charts. They can change the number of highways and develop charts for numbers multiplied by four and five.

Name _____ Date _____

Highways and Byways

Directions: Use craft sticks to make highways and byways that cross each other. Record the number of highways, byways, and signal lights you use. Write the equations.

Highways	Byways	Signal Lights	Equation

Draw one of the maps you made with craft sticks. Write a word problem about it for a classmate to solve.

_____

_____

_____

_____

_____

How Many Sides?

Standard
Geometry—Use visualization, spatial reasoning, and geometric modeling to solve problems.

Objective
Using square tiles, students will make shapes with different numbers of sides.

Materials
How Many Sides? reproducible
overhead projector

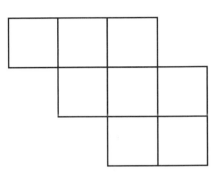

Challenge students to design different shapes using the same number of tiles. In this problem-solving activity, students use logical/mathematical skills to make designs and spatial skills to draw a representation of their shapes on graph paper.

Strategies
Problem-based learning

Cooperative group learning

1. Give each student a copy of the **How Many Sides? reproducible (page 22)**. Have students cut apart the eight tiles at the bottom of the worksheet.

2. Challenge students to use six of their tiles to design a shape and count the sides. Have students demonstrate their shapes on the overhead projector and count the sides together. Establish rules that the edges of the tiles must touch each other and that no shape can have a hole in it.

3. Divide the class into small groups of three or four. Challenge students to use all eight tiles to make shapes with a different number of sides and to make as many as they can. (Students should be able to design shapes with 4, 6, 8, 10, 12, 14, and 16 sides.)

4. Have each group share one piece of graph paper to record their shape configurations. Tell group members to draw and label their shapes to show the number of sides. They can do this by writing the number *1* by each side and then adding the total number of sides.

▶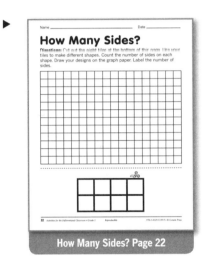

How Many Sides? Page 22

Ideas for More Differentiation
Students whose visual/spatial skills are less developed may have difficulty transferring shapes to the grid paper. Encourage them to trace around their designs on plain paper.

How Many Sides?

Directions: Cut out the eight tiles at the bottom of this page. Use your tiles to make different shapes. Count the number of sides on each shape. Draw your designs on the graph paper. Label the number of sides.

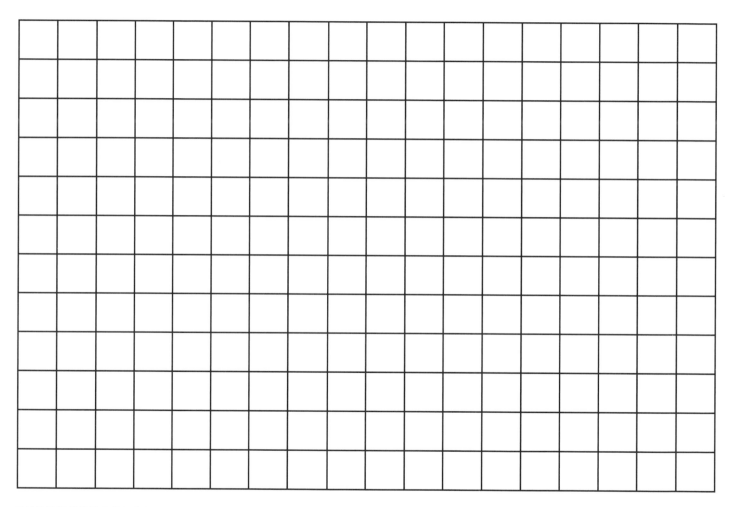

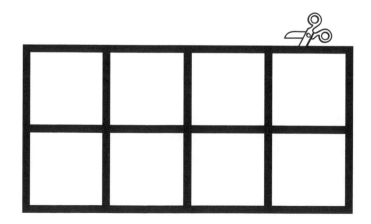

Follow the Bouncing Ball

Standard

Data Analysis and Probability—Formulate questions that can be addressed with data, and collect, organize, and display relevant even to answer them.

Objective

Students will make a line graph to show how the skill of bouncing a basketball improves over time.

Materials

Bouncing Ball Tally Chart reproducible
Bouncing Ball Line Graph reproducible
basketballs

Strategies

Authentic task

Cooperative group learning

This highly motivational activity invites students to work with a partner to record the number of times they dribble a basketball. They then graph their data to show if they improve over time. This activity builds on students' bodily/kinesthetic abilities.

1. Do the first part of this activity outdoors on a paved surface or in the gym. Before assigning partners, observe students as you give them the following instructions, and then pair them according to similar ability levels. Ask students to bounce the ball with their left hand; bounce the ball with their right hand; hold the ball with both hands; bounce it once, and catch it with their fingers; toss the ball over their head, and catch it without letting it bounce; and toss the ball up, clap once, and catch it.

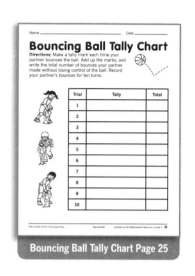

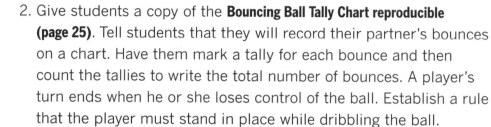

2. Give students a copy of the **Bouncing Ball Tally Chart reproducible (page 25)**. Tell students that they will record their partner's bounces on a chart. Have them mark a tally for each bounce and then count the tallies to write the total number of bounces. A player's turn ends when he or she loses control of the ball. Establish a rule that the player must stand in place while dribbling the ball.

3. Give each student ten turns to dribble the ball. Students can decide if they want to alternate after each turn or do all ten turns consecutively before their partner gets a turn. The object is to improve their score on each successive turn.

4. When students return to the classroom, have them analyze their data. Ask: *What was the highest number of bounces you made at one time? Did you get better with practice?* You might also discuss average, range, and mode if your students are already familiar with the terms.

Bouncing Ball Tally Chart Page 25

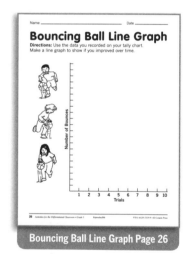

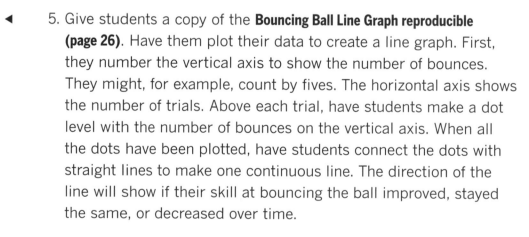

5. Give students a copy of the **Bouncing Ball Line Graph reproducible (page 26)**. Have them plot their data to create a line graph. First, they number the vertical axis to show the number of bounces. They might, for example, count by fives. The horizontal axis shows the number of trials. Above each trial, have students make a dot level with the number of bounces on the vertical axis. When all the dots have been plotted, have students connect the dots with straight lines to make one continuous line. The direction of the line will show if their skill at bouncing the ball improved, stayed the same, or decreased over time.

Ideas for More Differentiation

Encourage students with bodily/kinesthetic learning styles to create other line graphs for the number of jumps they can complete with a jump rope or the number of times they can bounce a ping-pong ball on a table using just the paddle.

Bouncing Ball Line Graph Page 26

978-1-4129-5339-9 • © Corwin Press

Bouncing Ball Tally Chart

Directions: Make a tally mark each time your partner bounces the ball. Add up the marks, and write the total number of bounces your partner made without losing control of the ball. Record your partner's bounces for ten turns.

Trial	Tally	Total
1		
2		
3		
4		
5		
6		
7		
8		
9		
10		

Bouncing Ball Line Graph

Directions: Use the data you recorded on your tally chart.
Make a line graph to show if you improved over time.

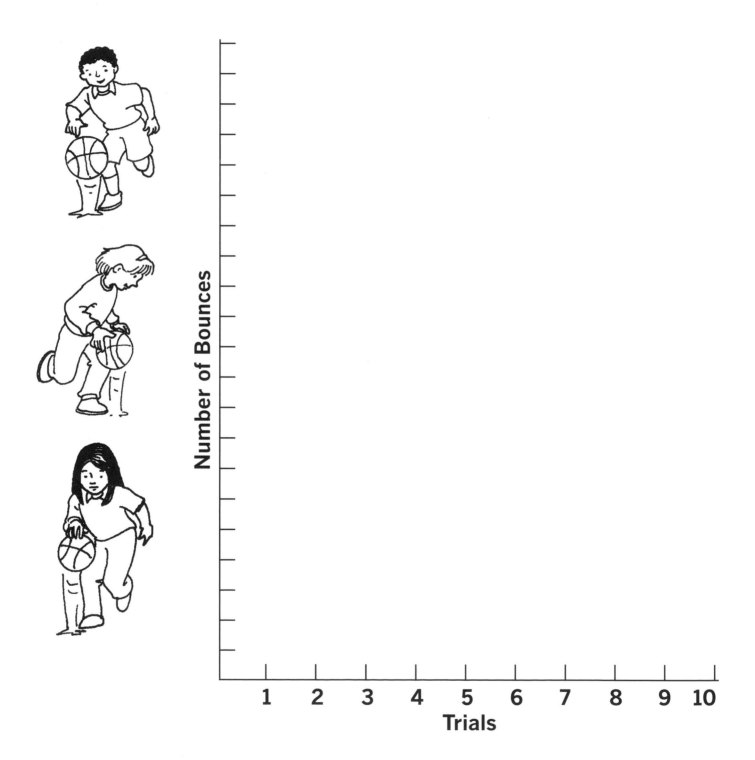

Number of Bounces

1   2   3   4   5   6   7   8   9   10

Trials

Eat Your Fruits and Veggies!

Standard
Problem Solving—Apply and adapt a variety of appropriate strategies to solve problems.

Objective
Students will use a guess-check-revise method to solve problems.

Materials
Fruits and Veggies Picture Cards reproducible
Fruits and Veggies Problem Cards reproducible
Fruits and Veggies Chart reproducible
colored pocket folders (red, green, blue)

In this structured center activity, students select a level 1, 2, or 3 problem and use a guess-check-revise method to solve it.

1. Prepare three colored pocket folders in red, green, and blue. In each folder, place several copies of the **Fruits and Veggies Picture Cards** and **Fruits and Veggies Chart (pages 30–31)**. Then reproduce several copies of the **Fruits and Veggies Problem Cards (page 29)**. Cut apart the cards, and place several copies of each problem-solving card in the corresponding colored folder.

2. Based on your observations of students' problem-solving skills and the level of difficulty of the problem in each folder, assign individual students to complete the problem in the red (level 1), green (level 2), or blue (level 3) folder.

3. Invite students to cut apart the fruit and vegetable cards and use them to solve the problem in the folder. Once students have solved the problem, have them glue the fruit and vegetable cards in place on the worksheet, explain their answer, and staple their problem-solving card to the worksheet.

Red
The students in Mr. Meatloaf's class are learning to eat more fruits and vegetables. Their assignment is to eat 24 servings of fruits and vegetables over the next four days. Dylan decided to eat the same number of servings each day. How many did he eat on Tuesday, Wednesday, Thursday, and Friday?
(Answer: Tuesday–6, Wednesday–6, Thursday–6, Friday–6)

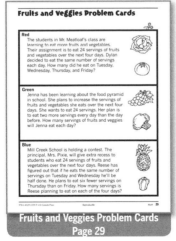

Fruits and Veggies Chart Page 31

Fruits and Veggies Problem Cards Page 29

Green

Jenna has been learning about the food pyramid in school. She plans to increase the servings of fruits and vegetables she eats over the next four days. She wants to eat 24 servings. Her plan is to eat two more servings every day than the day before. How many servings of fruits and veggies will Jenna eat each day?

(Answer: first day, 3 servings; second day, 5 servings or 3 + 2; third day, 7 servings or 5 + 2; fourth day, 9 servings or 7 + 2. Total = 3 + 5 + 7 + 9 = 24 servings)

Blue

Mill Creek School is holding a contest. The principal, Mrs. Pixie, will give extra recess to students who eat 24 servings of fruits and vegetables over the next four days. Reese has figured out that if he eats the same number of servings on Tuesday and Wednesday he'll be half done. He plans to eat six fewer servings on Thursday than on Friday. How many servings is Reese planning to eat on each of the four days?

(Answer: Reese eats 6 servings on Tuesday and Wednesday [6 + 6 = 12] or half of 24. He eats 3 servings on Thursday and 9 servings on Friday. 3 + 9 = 12, 12 + 12 = 24 servings)

Ideas for More Differentiation

Place other leveled word problems in the colored folders. Change them each week, and add them to your classroom math center.

Fruits and Veggies Problem Cards

Red

The students in Mr. Meatloaf's class are learning to eat more fruits and vegetables. Their assignment is to eat 24 servings of fruits and vegetables over the next four days. Dylan decided to eat the same number of servings each day. How many did he eat on Tuesday, Wednesday, Thursday, and Friday?

Green

Jenna has been learning about the food pyramid in school. She plans to increase the servings of fruits and vegetables she eats over the next four days. She wants to eat 24 servings. Her plan is to eat two more servings every day than the day before. How many servings of fruits and veggies will Jenna eat each day?

Blue

Mill Creek School is holding a contest. The principal, Mrs. Pixie, will give extra recess to students who eat 24 servings of fruits and vegetables over the next four days. Reese has figured out that if he eats the same number of servings on Tuesday and Wednesday he'll be half done. He plans to eat six fewer servings on Thursday than on Friday. How many servings is Reese planning to eat on each of the four days?

Fruits and Veggies Picture Cards

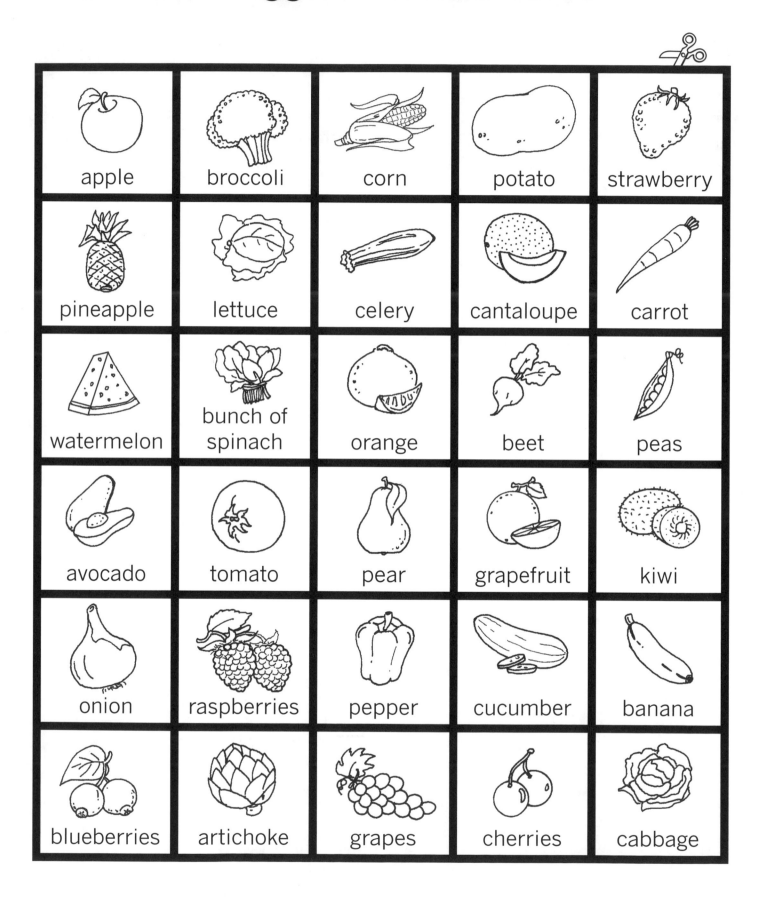

apple	broccoli	corn	potato	strawberry
pineapple	lettuce	celery	cantaloupe	carrot
watermelon	bunch of spinach	orange	beet	peas
avocado	tomato	pear	grapefruit	kiwi
onion	raspberries	pepper	cucumber	banana
blueberries	artichoke	grapes	cherries	cabbage

Name _____ Date _____

Fruits and Veggies Chart

Directions: Place your word problem next to the chart. Underline what you know. Circle what you need to find out. Use the fruit and vegetable cards to solve your problem, and glue them to the chart. Explain your answer below.

Tuesday	Wednesday	Thursday	Friday

Explain your answer. _____

_____

Scientific Observation

Strategies
Sponge activity

Focus activity

Standard
Science in Personal and Social Perspectives—Understand changes in environments.

Objective
Students will closely observe changes in the environment.

As you begin a unit on changes in the environment, focus students' attention on how to observe, an important skill for scientists. The following game will challenge students' creativity and observation skills.

1. Divide the class into two teams—Changers and Observers.

2. Set a timer for five minutes. Ask Observers to leave the room and take a book with them so they can read during this time.

3. Invite Changers to make changes to the classroom environment while Observers are away. Changers can make changes in what they are wearing or in the environment. For example, they might trade a shoe with someone or put a jacket on backwards. They might remove a poster from a wall or turn the teacher's chair.

4. When five minutes are up, invite Observers to return to the classroom. Set the timer for five minutes again, and challenge them to look for things that have changed. For every change they spot, they earn one point. Keep track of points on the board. Make the game more challenging by subtracting a point for each unrecognized change.

5. Have the class put everything back in order and then switch roles so each team has an opportunity to be both Changers and Observers.

Ideas for More Differentiation
Students with strong spatial skills will enjoy drawing a picture containing three or four out-of-place things. Display the pictures on a bulletin board with a file folder pocket containing slips of paper. Encourage students to list the mistakes they see in the pictures.

Research Probe: A Famous Scientist

Standard
History and Nature of Science—Understand science as a human endeavor.

Objective
Students will research and create a probe report about a famous scientist.

Materials
Famous Scientists reproducible
Famous Scientist Research Probe reproducible
Famous Scientist Rubric reproducible
paper lunch bag
poster board, art supplies
research materials, such as books and the Internet

This activity allows students to apply their verbal/linguistic and spatial skills while also encouraging those with naturalist intelligence. Students research a famous scientist and create an all-in-one report displayed on a poster. The report combines both text and visuals.

1. Give students an opportunity to delve into the lives of famous scientists. Make a copy of the **Famous Scientists reproducible (page 35)**. Cut apart the scientists' names, and place them in a paper bag. Invite each student to draw one name from the bag. This is the scientist they will research.

2. After students have selected scientists, provide time in class for research, or invite students to do research as a homework assignment over several weeks. For students with limited resources, consider loaning them books or materials printed from the Internet.

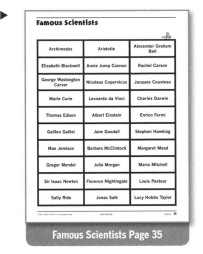

Famous Scientists Page 35

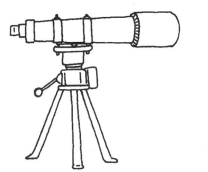

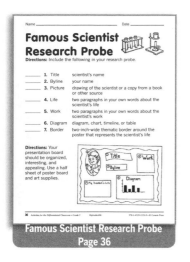

Famous Scientist Research Probe
Page 36

3. Give each student a copy of the **Famous Scientist Research Probe** and **Famous Scientist Rubric reproducibles (pages 36–37)** and a half sheet of poster board. You will use the rubric to grade students' probes. (The rubric is open-ended to accommodate a variety of grading systems. Assign number values to each element to emphasize your teaching priorities.)

4. Have students research the following probe elements and include the information on their posters. Encourage them to use separate pieces of paper to record the research for each probe element and then glue the papers onto their poster.

   Title: scientist's name

   Byline: student's name

   Picture: picture of the scientist (hand-drawn or a copy from a book)

   Life: two paragraphs about the scientist's life (handwritten clearly or typed)

   Work: two paragraphs about the scientist's work

   Diagram: diagram of something that was an important part of the scientist's work (hand-drawn or copied)

   Border: two-inch-wide border around the poster to represent a theme of the scientist's life

5. Encourage students to be creative and make their posters colorful and appealing. Remind them that written text must be in their own words. They must not copy any published work.

6. Laminate the finished probe reports to protect them, and create a display for your and other classes to tour and enjoy. This display is great for an open house!

Ideas for More Differentiation

Have students present their reports orally. This provides students with strong verbal abilities an alternate way to share what they learned. Give students index cards to take notes for their presentation, and provide an easel or chalkboard ledge to display the posters.

Famous Scientists

Archimedes	Aristotle	Alexander Graham Bell
Elizabeth Blackwell	Annie Jump Cannon	Rachel Carson
George Washington Carver	Nicolaus Copernicus	Jacques Cousteau
Marie Curie	Leonardo da Vinci	Charles Darwin
Thomas Edison	Albert Einstein	Enrico Fermi
Galileo Galilei	Jane Goodall	Stephen Hawking
Mae Jemison	Barbara McClintock	Margaret Mead
Gregor Mendel	Julia Morgan	Maria Mitchell
Sir Isaac Newton	Florence Nightingale	Louis Pasteur
Sally Ride	Jonas Salk	Lucy Hobbs Taylor

Name _____   Date _____

Famous Scientist Research Probe

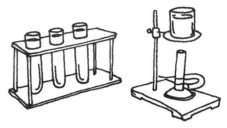

Directions: Include the following in your research probe.

_____	**1.** Title	scientist's name
_____	**2.** Byline	your name
_____	**3.** Picture	drawing of the scientist or a copy from a book or other source
_____	**4.** Life	two paragraphs in your own words about the scientist's life
_____	**5.** Work	two paragraphs in your own words about the scientist's work
_____	**6.** Diagram	diagram, chart, timeline, or table
_____	**7.** Border	two-inch-wide thematic border around the poster that represents the scientist's life

Directions: Your presentation board should be organized, interesting, and appealing. Use a half sheet of poster board and art supplies.

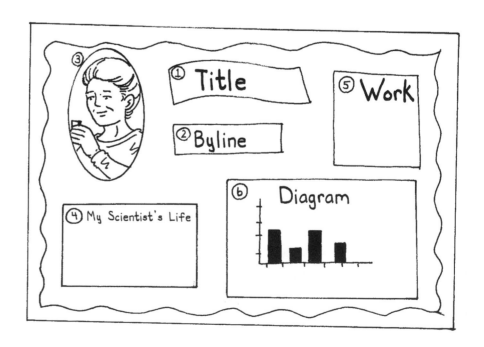

Famous Scientist Rubric

Name: _____ Date: _____

Grade: ▢

Poster includes:

_____ title and byline

_____ scientist's picture

_____ two paragraphs about the scientist's life in your own words

_____ two paragraphs about the scientist's work in your own words

_____ diagram, chart, timeline, or table

_____ thematic border

Total points for written report: ▢

Oral report was:

_____ spoken, not read

_____ well-organized

_____ well-prepared

_____ delivered with good eye contact

_____ delivered in a voice that everyone can hear

Total points for oral report: ▢

Weather Rotation

Strategies

Rotation reflection

Rehearsal

Standard

Earth and Space Science—Understand changes in the earth and sky.

Objective

Students will rotate through stations to reflect on what they have learned about weather.

Materials

chart paper
colored markers

This review activity will help students rehearse what they have learned during a weather study unit. It gives them the opportunity to work in small groups and to circulate around the room—an effective strategy for students with interpersonal and bodily/kinesthetic learning styles.

1. Select five or six weather-related topics you wish students to review, such as clouds, tornadoes, hurricanes, temperature, rain, snow, or thunderstorms. Label several sheets of chart paper with one topic each.

2. Place the charts at stations around the room. Divide the class into small groups, and give each group a marker of a different color. Instruct groups to use only their own color. This will allow you to keep track of each group's contributions.

3. Assign each group to a chart, and instruct them to brainstorm as many facts about their topic as they can. Have each group determine who will be the recorder and will write the facts on the chart paper. After a short time, give a signal for groups to stop and move to the next chart. Have groups do the same for the new topic. Continue rotating until each group has added information to every chart in their own color.

4. Have each group share the information from their final chart. Invite the class to listen carefully and add important information or correct any misinformation.

Ideas for More Differentiation

This follow-up activity helps spatial learners reinforce what they have learned. Have students select a chart topic and illustrate and label one of the facts. Assemble the illustrations from each chart into a book for the class library.

Bird Beaks

Standard
Life Science—Understand characteristics of organisms.

Objective
Students will investigate types of bird beaks and compare them to the birds' feeding habits.

Materials
Bird Beaks reproducible
Rainforest Birds by Bobbie Kalman
"bird beaks" (tweezers, clip-on clothespins, plastic spoons, pliers)
"bird food" (pumpkin seeds, marbles, toothpicks, plastic or
gummy bugs, pennies, washers)
small plastic trays
small paper cups

Strategies
Analogy

Graphic organizer

Use this small-group activity to accompany a study of birds or animal adaptations. This motivating, hands-on exploration engages students with naturalist as well as bodily/kinesthetic learning styles.

Develop background knowledge for this activity by sharing with the class some books about birds, such as *Rainforest Birds* by Bobbie Kalman, and Internet resources about types of bird beaks, such as The Norman Bird Sanctuary Web: Bird Adaptations: Beaks at *www.normanbirdsanctuary.com/beak_adaptations.shtml*.

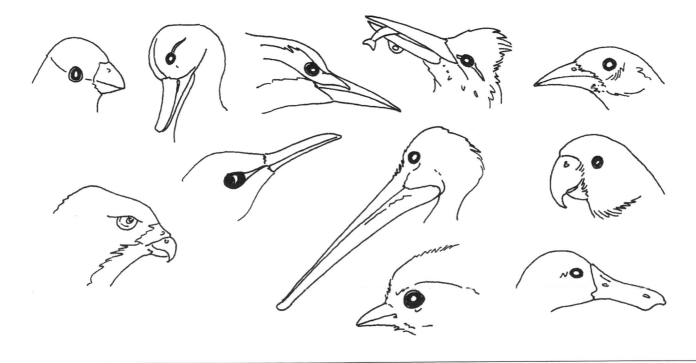

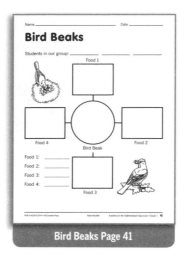

Bird Beaks Page 41

1. Divide the class into groups of three. Give each student a copy of the **Bird Beaks reproducible (page 41)** and a paper cup. Invite each group to select three "bird beaks" (tweezers, clothespin, plastic spoon, or pliers). Then ask each group member to draw a picture of one type of bird beak in the center of the graphic organizer.

2. Provide each group with a small tray of four kinds of "bird food" (pumpkin seeds, marbles, toothpicks, plastic bugs, pennies, or washers). Instruct students to write the name of or draw each type of food in a section of their graphic organizer.

3. Have the first student in each group use a bird beak to pick up and place in a cup as many pieces of bird food as possible during a one-minute time period. Have him or her count the number of each food type and record it in the corresponding section on the graphic organizer. Have the second and third students repeat the activity using different bird beaks.

4. Have students compare their graphic organizers and draw conclusions about which type of bird beak works or does not work for different kinds of food. Ask students what conclusions they can draw about birds from this activity. Use the following prompts:

    • *Were you able to pick up all kinds of foods equally well with all kinds of beaks?* (Most likely not.)

    • *Do birds with different types of beaks eat the same types of food?* (No, their beaks are adapted to the type of food. The size and shape of a bird's beak determine what it eats.)

    • *Could this have an effect on the variety of birds that can be found in one area?* (Yes, because many kinds of birds can live in one area where there is a variety of food available.)

Ideas for More Differentiation

Provide a variety of bird photos collected from books or Internet sources. Invite students with naturalist learning styles to identify different types of tail feathers and feet. Have students draw some of them. Challenge students to combine beaks, tails, and feet to create an original bird and give it a name.

978-1-4129-5339-9

Name _____   Date _____

Bird Beaks

Students in our group: _____ _____ _____

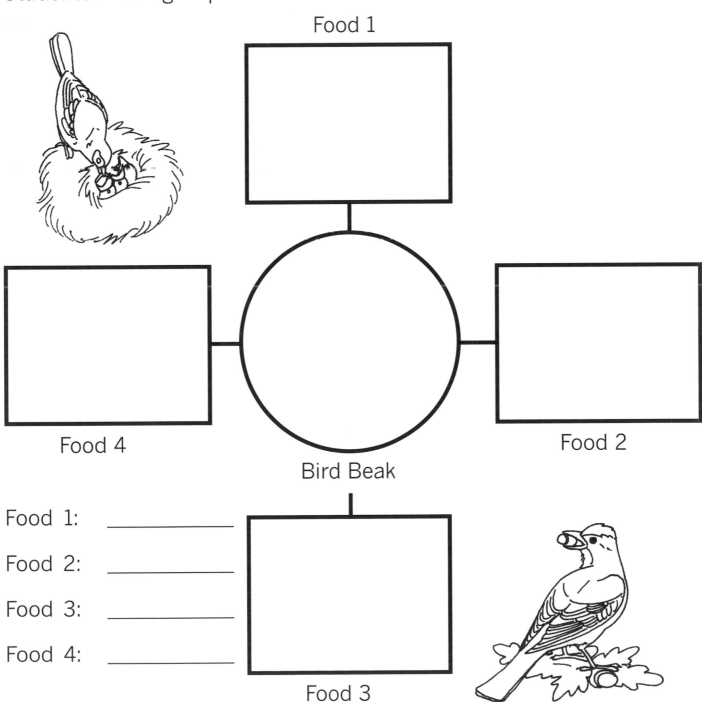

Food 1

Food 4

Bird Beak

Food 2

Food 3

Food 1: _____

Food 2: _____

Food 3: _____

Food 4: _____

Leaf Classification

Strategies

Authentic task

Reflection after learning

Standard

Science as Inquiry—Ability to conduct scientific inquiry.

Objective

Students will establish a classification system for leaves.

Materials

Leaf Classification reproducible
leaves and needles (assorted colors, shapes, and sizes)

This authentic inquiry engages naturalist, interpersonal, and verbal/linguistic learning styles. Invite students to assemble a leaf collection and make decisions about classification. Through observation and hands-on experience, they will learn about variety in nature and hierarchies in classification systems.

1. Ask students to collect many different kinds of leaves and needles from trees and other plants. Spread the collection on a table so everyone can see. Invite students to examine the collection closely and brainstorm some characteristics that might allow the leaves to be classified into groups. Use the following prompts to encourage close observation:

   - *Does each needle join a main stem or branch out from smaller ones?*

   - *Are needles sharp or soft?*

   - *Are needles stiff or bendable?*

   - *Are leaves simple or do they have several leaflets?*

   - *Are leaves smooth-edged or toothed?*

   - *Are leaves feathery or finger-like?*

   - *Can leaves be grouped by color?*

   - *Are some leaves broad and others slim?*

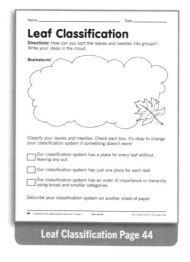

Leaf Classification Page 44

2. Give students a copy of the **Leaf Classification reproducible (page 44)**. As you conduct this discussion, invite students to record key words and ideas in the brainstorming cloud.

3. Explain that a classification system is what scientists use to organize and order what they observe in nature. Tell students they will create a classification system for the leaf and needle collection. Give students the following characteristics of an effective classification system:

   • works for every specimen

   • will change as ideas are tested

   • ensures that each specimen will fit in only one place

   • is hierarchical

4. Continue that a hierarchical system includes both broad and small categories. The smaller categories are subsets of the broad ones. For example, vehicles can be grouped into two broad categories, trucks and cars. Each of these broad categories can be divided into several smaller categories. The broad category *trucks* can be divided into pick-ups, SUVs, semis, and haulers. The broad category *cars* can be divided into hatchbacks, sedans, compacts, and station wagons.

5. Divide the class into small groups, and give each group an assortment of leaves and needles from the class collection. Invite groups to establish a classification system that works for their collection using their notes from the class discussion. Visual learners may benefit from drawing a diagram of the classification system on the back of the worksheet.

6. Invite students to share their classification system with the class. They can check off the boxes on their worksheet for each criterion met. Provide students time to reflect and write a description of their classification system.

Ideas for More Differentiation

Start a collection of pinecones at a science center. Encourage students to contribute to it. As the collection grows, invite students to classify and reclassify the collection, adjusting for new specimens. Ask them to describe their classification system or draw a diagram in their journals.

Name _____ Date _____

Leaf Classification

Directions: How can you sort the leaves and needles into groups? Write your ideas in the cloud.

Brainstorm!

Classify your leaves and needles. Check each box. It's okay to change your classification system if something doesn't work!

☐ Our classification system has a place for every leaf without leaving any out.

☐ Our classification system has just one place for each leaf.

☐ Our classification system has an order of importance or hierarchy using broad and smaller categories.

Describe your classification system on another sheet of paper.

Out in Space

Standard
Earth and Space Science—Identify objects in the sky.

Objective
Students will identify objects in space.

Materials
Out in Space Riddles reproducibles
Out in Space reproducible
tape

This game gives students an opportunity to review what they know about objects in space while moving around the room, which is especially appealing to bodily/kinesthetic learners. Interpersonal learners will enjoy interacting with others to complete their lists, while intrapersonal learners will enjoy meeting the individual challenge.

1. Make enough copies of the **Out in Space Riddles reproducibles (pages 46–47)** so that you have a riddle for each student. Cut apart and distribute the riddles, and ask students to keep their riddle a secret. Have students write their name on the back of their riddle and cut off the answer section. They can keep the answer in their pocket or desk. Then tape the riddles to students' backs.

2. Give students a copy of the **Out in Space reproducible (page 48)**. The object of the game is to read the riddles on other students' backs and find one riddle about each object on the list. After students read a riddle, they can ask the student wearing it: *Are you (name of object)?* If they are correct, they write the student's name on their list next to the name of the object.

3. Give a signal for students to get out of their seats, and begin the game. After five minutes, tell students the time is up. Have each student read their riddle and reveal their object's name so others can complete their lists.

Out in Space Page 48

Ideas for More Differentiation
Encourage verbal/linguistic learners to research and write clues for other science topics, such as constellations, animals, or plants. Then invite the class to play the game again using new topics.

Out in Space Riddles

 I am a ball of very hot gases.

I am bigger than any planet in our solar system.

I give off huge amounts of energy.

Answer: Sun

 I am an inner planet.

I am the closest planet to the sun.

My surface is covered with craters.

Answer: Mercury

 I am an inner planet.

My atmosphere has thick clouds of sulfuric acid.

I am the second planet from the sun.

Answer: Venus

 I look like a blue ball with white swirls around it.

I can support life.

I have water, air, and moderate temperatures.

Answer: Earth

 I am covered with red rocks and dust.

I am an inner planet.

I have craters and huge extinct volcanoes.

Answer: Mars

 I am a fast-spinning planet.

I am the largest planet in our solar system.

My Great Red Spot is probably a huge storm.

Answer: Jupiter

Out in Space Riddles

 I am a giant planet.

I have thousands of shiny rings.

I also have at least 37 moons.

Answer: Saturn

 I am a giant planet of gases.

It takes me 84 Earth years to orbit the sun.

I rotate in a tilted position.

Answer: Uranus

 I am an outer planet.

I have rings and a Great Dark Spot.

I am named after the Roman god of the sea.

Answer: Neptune

I am a dwarf planet.

Some scientists say I am not a real planet.

I make an oval-shaped path around the sun.

Answer: Pluto

 I am the brightest object in the night sky.

My light comes from the sun.

I was the first object in space to be visited by people from Earth.

Answer: the Moon

 We are pieces of rock and metal.

Most of us are grouped in a belt between Mars and Jupiter.

Ceres is the largest one of us.

Answer: asteroids

Out in Space

Directions: Find someone who is wearing a riddle that describes each space object. Write the person's name next to the object.

Space Object	Student's Name
1. Asteroid	_____
2. Earth	_____
3. Jupiter	_____
4. Mars	_____
5. Mercury	_____
6. the Moon	_____
7. Pluto	_____
8. Saturn	_____
9. the Sun	_____
10. Uranus	_____
11. Venus	_____

Focus on Static Electricity

Standard
Physical Science—Understand light, heat, electricity, and magnetism.

Objective
Students will explore static electricity.

Materials
shallow, clear plastic food storage containers with lids
wool, nylon, or fur pieces
puffed rice cereal
construction paper

Strategies
Focus activity

Problem-based learning

Use this hands-on focus activity to introduce students to electricity. Especially appealing to logical/mathematical and tactile learners, this activity allows students to observe static electricity and solve a problem.

1. Divide the class into small groups of three or four. Give each group a food container holding some puffed rice cereal; a piece of wool, nylon, or fur; and a construction paper work mat.

2. Present the following problem: *Move the puffed rice to your work mat using a piece of material. You must do it without touching the cereal with your hands and without pouring it. Count the number of pieces you are able to move.*

3. If after several minutes students have difficulty coming up with a solution, ask them if they have ever rubbed an inflated balloon on their clothing and then held it near their hair. Lead them to discover that rubbing the lid of the container causes the cereal inside to jump to the lid. (Some also jumps off again.) Rubbing a balloon and rubbing the container lid creates static electricity that attracts or repels other objects.

4. Extend this activity by having students rub the bottom of the container and then place cereal in it. Instruct them to move their finger under the container and watch what happens. The cereal puffs will hop around or fly off.

Ideas for More Differentiation
Encourage students with linguistic skills to write their observations in their journals. Ask them to write three questions about what they observed. As you continue your study of electricity, tell students to write the answers to their questions.

CHAPTER 3

Social Studies

Map Making

Strategies
Structured project

Jigsaw

Standard
Understand the interactions among people, places, and environments.

Objective
Students will create a bulletin board about maps.

Materials
Map Making reproducible
white butcher paper
sentence strips
index cards
markers
stapler

Use this activity to introduce students to map skills. Tailor the activity to accommodate the number of students in your class. Everyone has an opportunity to contribute to the final product.

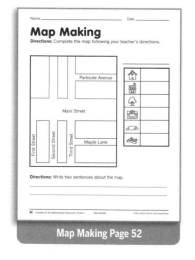

Map Making Page 52

1. Cover a bulletin board with white butcher paper. Enlarge the **Map Making reproducible (page 52)** to fit your bulletin board space, and trace it on the prepared area.

2. Prepare the following 26 word, phrase, and symbol cards by writing each on a sentence strip or index card. Adjust the number of pieces if you have fewer or more students by lengthening or shortening some of the phrases so there is a word, phrase, or symbol card for each student.

   Write in black: Oak City, Map Key, house, school, airport, park, mall, pond,

   Write in red: A symbol, is anything, that, stands for, something, else.

   Write in blue: A map, key, helps us, understand, the symbols, on a map.

   Draw these symbols from the map key on index cards: house, school, airport, park, mall, pond

3. Give each student a word, phrase, or symbol card. Ask students questions that can be answered by the cards they hold, such as: *Who has a title for the map?* (Oak City) *Who has a title for the chart that shows symbols?* (Map Key) *Who has the name for this symbol?* (Point to a symbol on the Map Key.) Invite students holding the appropriate cards to staple them to the bulletin board.

4. Invite students holding symbol cards to place them on the bulletin board following your description of each location.

    • *The school is north of Parkside Ave. and east of Third St.*

    • *The mall is north of Main St. between First St. and Second St.*

    • *The park is south of Parkside Ave. and north of Main St.*

    • *The airport is south of Main St. between First St. and Second St.*

    • *The pond is south of Main St. between Second St. and Third St.*

    • *There is a house south of Maple Ln. and east of Third St.*

5. Ask students with red cards to stand in front of the class. Have them figure out how to arrange themselves to make a sentence: *A symbol is anything that stands for something else.* Staple the sentence to the bulletin board.

6. Ask students with blue cards to stand and do the same. *A map key helps us understand the symbols on a map.*

7. Give students a copy of the Map Making reproducible. Invite them to complete their maps and write the sentences at the bottom using the bulletin board as a guide.

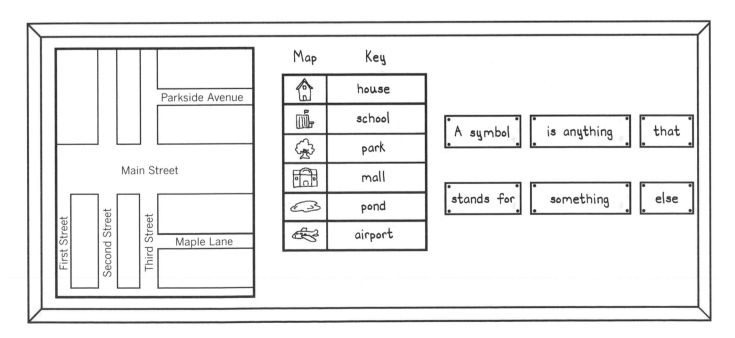

Name _____   Date _____

Map Making

Directions: Complete the map following your teacher's directions.

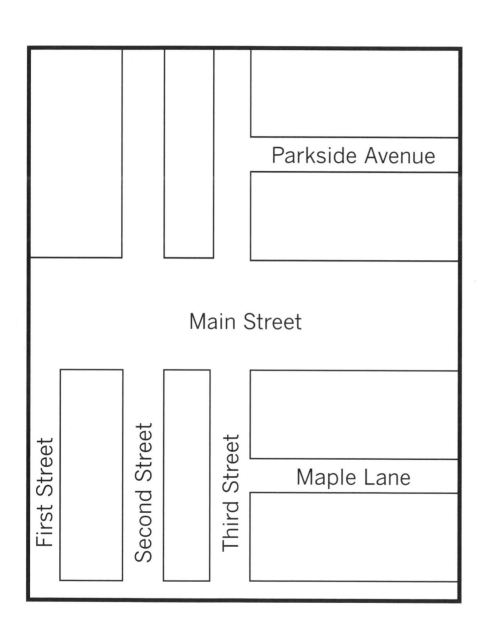

Directions: Write two sentences about the map.

_____

_____

Looking at Landforms

Standard
Understand the interactions among people, places, and environments.

Objective
Students will create models of landforms.

Materials
Looking at Landforms reproducible
modeling clay in several colors
clean frozen-food trays

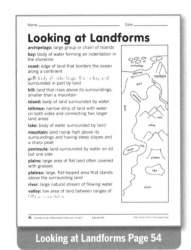
This small-group activity encourages students to share what they have learned about landforms. They apply their knowledge to create a model while developing interpersonal and spatial skills. Manipulating clay is a pleasurable tactile experience students never outgrow!

1. Divide the class into groups of three. Give each group member a different color of clay. Provide the group with a small, plastic frozen-food tray.

2. Give students a copy of the **Looking at Landforms reproducible (page 54)**. Review the landforms with the class. Invite each group to choose three landforms to include in their model. Explain that each student will contribute a landform but that the landforms must all flow together. In other words, each group will make a landscape, not simply three separate forms.

3. When students have completed their clay landscapes, have them make tent-shaped paper signs to label the landforms. Invite each group to present its landscape to the class. Place the landscapes on a display table with a sign listing group members' names.

Ideas for More Differentiation
Bodily/kinesthetic learners will enjoy working in groups of four or five. Have each group cooperatively create different landforms with their bodies. Call out one landform at a time challenge each group to work together to create it.

Name _____   Date _____

Looking at Landforms

archipelago: large group or chain of islands

bay: body of water forming an indentation in the shoreline

coast: edge of land that borders the ocean along a continent

gulf: body of water larger than a bay and surrounded in part by land

hill: land that rises above its surroundings, smaller than a mountain

island: body of land surrounded by water

isthmus: narrow strip of land with water on both sides and connecting two larger land areas

lake: body of water surrounded by land

mountain: land rising high above its surroundings and having steep slopes and a sharp peak

peninsula: land surrounded by water on all but one side

plains: large area of flat land often covered with grasses

plateau: large, flat-topped area that stands above the surrounding land

river: large natural stream of flowing water

valley: low area of land between ranges of hills or mountains

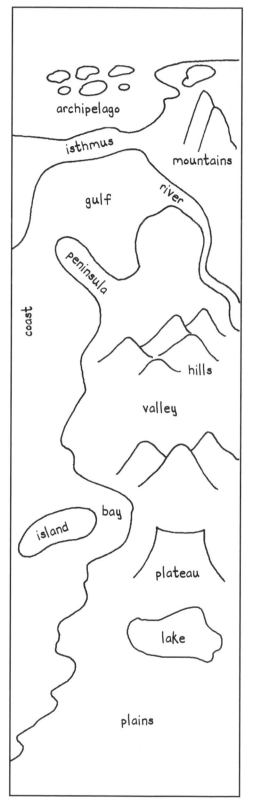

Famous United States Symbols

Standard
Understand the ideals, principles, and practices of citizenship in a democratic republic.

Objective
Students will identify United States landmarks and symbols.

Materials
United States Symbols reproducibles
tape

In this fun activity, students enjoy a guessing game of interpersonal interactions and movement. They use questioning techniques and deductive reasoning to identify famous United States symbols.

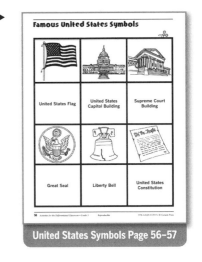

1. Make copies of the **United States Symbols reproducibles (pages 56–57)**. Cut apart the cards so you have a picture or word card for each student. Tape one card to each student's back without telling the student what it is.

2. Tell students they will ask each other questions to determine what picture or word is taped to their back. All questions must require only a *yes* or *no* answer. For example, students might ask: *Am I a monument? Am I in Washington D.C.? Am I a president? Am I the Lincoln Memorial?* At your signal, invite students to move around the room and ask questions.

3. For each picture there is a matching name card. After students figure out what is taped to their back, challenge them to find their matching classmate. After partners find each other, have them sit down together. When everyone is matched, have partners show and tell the class what they are.

United States Symbols Page 56–57

Ideas for More Differentiation
Challenge logical/mathematical and spatial learners to use the cards on the United States Symbols reproducible to play a *Concentration*-type memory game. Students place all the cards facedown and take turns turning over two cards at a time. If the cards match, the player keeps the cards. If they do not match, the player turns them facedown again. When all the cards are matched, players count the number of matches they made.

Famous United States Symbols

United States Flag	**United States Capitol Building**	**Supreme Court Building**
Great Seal	**Liberty Bell**	**United States Constitution**

Famous United States Symbols

Washington Monument	**Lincoln Memorial**	**White House**
Jefferson Memorial	**Statue of Liberty**	**Mount Rushmore**

Be an Explorer

Standard
Understand the ways human beings view themselves in and over time.

Objective
Students will conduct research and share an interesting discovery.

Materials
reference books

When you have a few minutes of class time to fill, engage students' verbal/linguistic abilities with this quick sponge activity. This activity appears simple but actually provides an exciting, creative challenge!

1. Make available a variety of reference books, such as nonfiction books, dictionaries, atlases, geography books, history books, and encyclopedias.

2. Invite students to work with a partner. Give each pair a book, and challenge them to find an interesting fact they did not know.

3. After students have had time to do some research, prompt students: *Tell us something we don't know.* Invite each pair to tell the class about their interesting discovery.

Ideas for More Differentiation
Invite independent learners to search for their discovery and then write about it or draw it in their journals.

Design a Postage Stamp

Standard
Understand how people create and change structures of power, authority, and governance.

Strategy
Open-ended project

Objective
Students will design postage stamps about a state.

Materials
Design a Postage Stamp reproducible
black construction paper
crayons or markers
yarn

Exercise students' visual/spatial skills with an activity that requires them to research and synthesize information about a state. After discovering important facts about a state, they will choose one visual design to represent it.

1. Invite students to bring in cancelled stamps to show the variety of postage stamps issued by the federal post office. Display them for the class. Have a discussion about the elements of a postage stamp. For example, most stamps have the letters *USA* and an amount printed on them. Discuss the artwork and subjects on the stamps. If possible, invite a philatelist to share his or her hobby with students.

2. Give students a copy of the **Design a Stamp reproducible (page 60)**. Assign each student a state to research. Have students select something that represents their assigned state to create a postage stamp design. They might select a state tree, bird, flower, or product to decorate their stamp. Other choices might include a significant person born in the state or an historical event that took place there.

3. Frame each completed stamp with black construction paper. Display the framed stamps on a bulletin board around a map of the United States. Use yarn to connect each stamp to its state on the map.

Design a Stamp Page 60

Ideas for More Differentiation
Encourage verbal/linguistic learners to write three facts about their assigned state before choosing a design. Taking notes helps students organize their thinking.

Design a Postage Stamp

Directions: Research some facts about your state. Select something that represents your state to create a postage stamp design.

Pilgrim Life

Standard
Understand the ways human beings view themselves in and over time.

Objective
Students will compare their daily life with that of a Pilgrim or Wampanoag child in early America.

Materials
A Day in the Life reproducible
Sarah Morton's Day: A Day in the Life of a Pilgrim Girl by Kate Waters
Samuel Eaton's Day: A Day in the Life of a Pilgrim Boy by Kate Waters
Tapenum's Day: A Wampanoag Indian Boy in Pilgrim Times by Kate Waters

Use literature to take students on a virtual field trip through time to the days of the Pilgrims. Kate Waters' books depict the life of children in early 1600s America.

1. Read aloud one or more of the suggested titles by Kate Waters, and discuss them with the class. A glossary at the back of each book will help students with unfamiliar terms. The photos in each book also provide details about the daily life of the main characters.

2. Encourage students to draw comparisons between the lives of the children in the books and their own lives. Ask questions such as: *What did they wear? How did they get food? What was their home like? How did they learn? What were their responsibilities? What did they do for fun?*

3. Give students a copy of the **A Day in the Life reproducible (page 62)**. If you have multiple copies of the Kate Waters books, assign small groups to complete their Venn diagrams together. If not, use an overhead projector or whiteboard to complete it as a class. Have students find details in the book to contribute to the diagram.

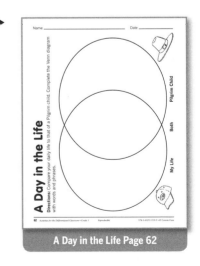

A Day in the Life Page 62

Ideas for More Differentiation
Bodily/kinesthetic learners will enjoy acting out the daily chores or other activities done by children from the 1600s. Challenge the class to guess which activity is being dramatized.

Name _____ Date _____

A Day in the Life

Directions: Compare your daily life to that of a Pilgrim child. Complete the Venn diagram with words and phrases.

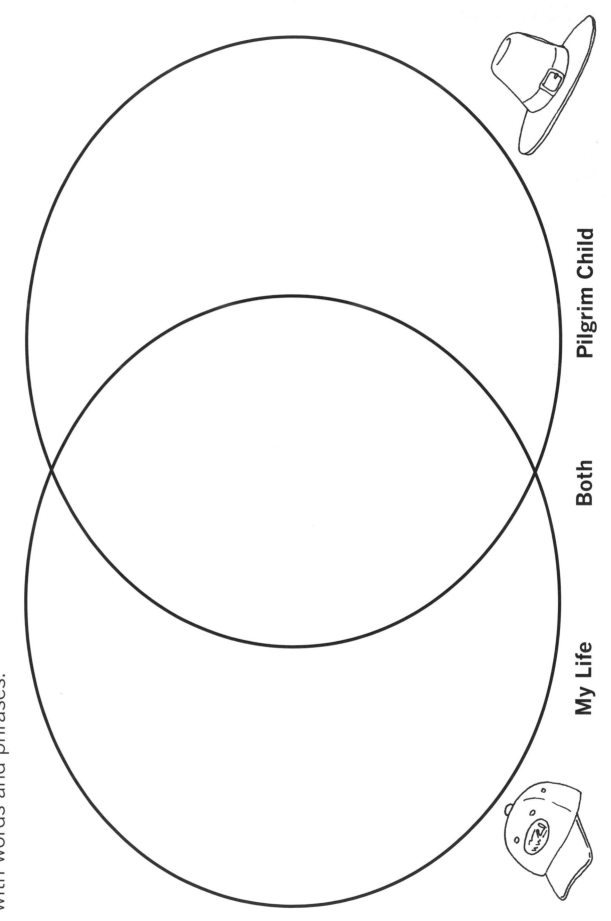

Pilgrim Child

Both

My Life

It's Constitution Day!

Standard
Understand the ideals, principles, and practices of citizenship in a democratic republic.

Strategies
Multiple intelligences

Mural

Objective
Students will learn the meaning of the Preamble to the United States Constitution and create a mural about it.

Materials
Constitution Preamble reproducible
We the Kids: The Preamble to the Constitution of the United States illustrated by David Catrow
reference materials
butcher paper, markers

Congress recently named September 17 Constitution Day and Citizenship Day. Schools receiving federal funds are required to educate students about the Constitution on this day. Invite students to interpret the Preamble to the U.S. Constitution and create a mural about it.

1. Read aloud *We the Kids,* which illustrates the Preamble to the Constitution. The preface and glossary are valuable tools for introducing the sophisticated ideas and language of the Preamble. As you read, give students plenty of time to discuss the meaning of the illustrations.

2. Divide the class into six small groups, and give each group a copy of the **Constitution Preamble reproducible (page 64)**. Focus on the five big ideas in the Preamble by highlighting one idea for each group to discuss: *We the People of the United States, establish justice, insure domestic tranquility, provide for the common defense, promote the general welfare, secure the blessings of liberty.*

3. Have students use reference materials to answer three questions about their big idea: *What does it mean? What is an example? Why is the idea important?* Have each group explain their answers.

4. Provide a large piece of butcher paper with phrases from the Preamble written at the top. Have each group illustrate their phrase. Display the mural in a school hallway.

Constitution Preamble

We The People

of the United States, in Order to form a more perfect Union, establish Justice, insure domestic Tranquility, provide for the common defense, promote the general Welfare, and secure the Blessings of Liberty to ourselves and our Posterity, do ordain and establish this Constitution for the United States of America.

Constitution Preamble Page 64

Constitution Preamble

We the People

of the United States, in Order
to form a more perfect Union,
establish Justice, insure
domestic Tranquility, provide for
the common defense, promote
the general Welfare, and secure
the Blessings of Liberty to
ourselves and our Posterity,
do ordain and establish this
Constitution for the
United States of America.

Continental Callout

Standard
Understand global connections and interdependence.

Objective
Students will identify the continents on a map.

Materials
Name the Continents reproducible
overhead projector
transparency

A quick geography rehearsal experience helps students memorize the locations of the continents. This sponge activity gives linguistic learners an opportunity to practice with paper and pencil.

1. Make a transparency of the **Name the Continents reproducible (page 66)**. Write a number on each continent. ▶

2. Every day when students enter the classroom, instruct them to number a sheet of paper from *1* to *7* and write the name of each continent beside its number. Take a moment to check answers together.

3. Change the numbers on the continents each day. Practicing over several days will help students master the continent locations. For a further challenge, modify the map to hide the names of the oceans, and have students identify them as well.

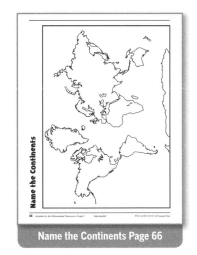

Name the Continents Page 66

Ideas for More Differentiation
Interpersonal learners will enjoy creating riddles about the locations of the continents and having the class guess the answers. For example: *I am a continent just south of Europe.* (Answer: Africa)

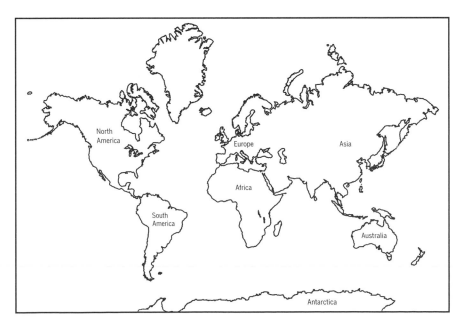

Name the Continents

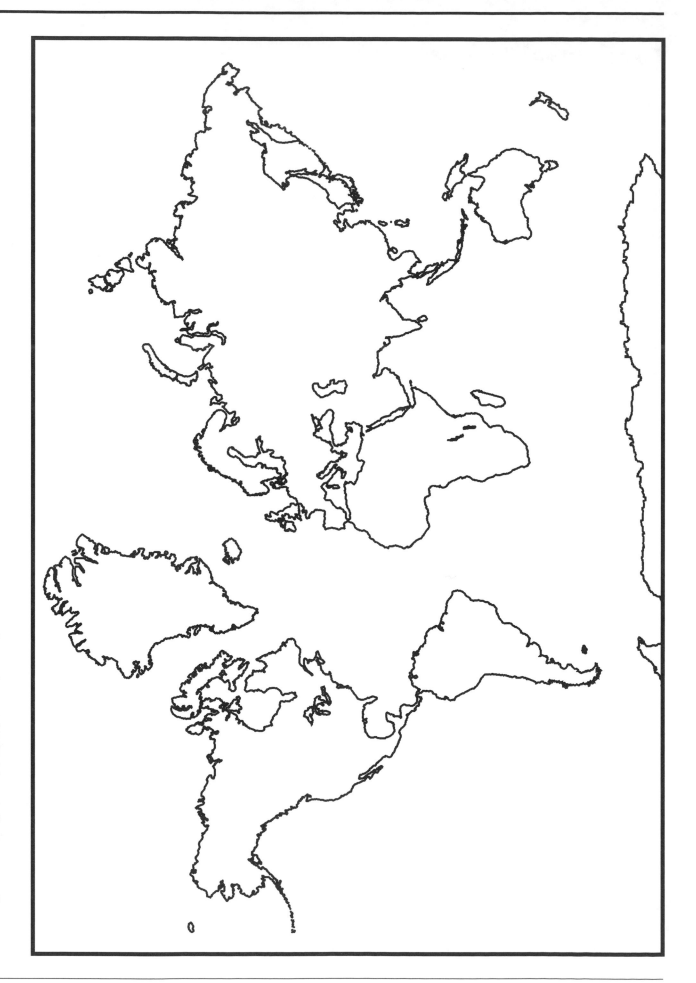

Reproducible 978-1-4129-5339-9 • © Corwin Press

CHAPTER 4

Language Arts

Describe a Character

Strategies

Graphic organizer

Cooperative group learning

Standard
Read a wide range of literature from many periods in many genres to build an understanding of the many dimensions (e.g., philosophical, ethical, aesthetic) of human experience.

Objective
Students will describe characters in a chapter book.

Materials
Describe a Character reproducible
index cards

Character study is one area of comprehension that grows in importance as students begin reading more complex chapter books independently. Encourage students to carefully consider the inner as well as outer attributes of book characters. Use this activity with a book the class is currently reading.

1. Write each major character's name on an index card. Divide the class into small groups according to the number of cards you made. Give one card to each group.

2. Explain to students that they will generate a list of descriptions about their character. Invite them to think about their character's outer features (appearance) as well as their character's inner features (thoughts and feelings). Interpersonal learners will enjoy the opportunity to discuss characters with the group. Students with linguistic strengths can serve as recorders.

3. Give each group a copy of the **Describe a Character reproducible (page 68)**. Establish a time limit. Invite the recorder to write the group's ideas in each category of the graphic organizer. Encourage groups to share their ideas with the class.

◄ **Describe a Character Page 68**

Ideas for More Differentiation
Ask students with visual/spatial learning styles to illustrate a character in a way that reveals his or her inner feelings.

Describe a Character

Directions: Work with your group to describe your book character. List the character's outer features (appearance) and inner features (thoughts and feelings).

Book Title: _____

Character: _____

Outer Features (Appearance)	Inner Features (Thoughts and Feelings)

Say It with a Storyboard

Standard

Apply a wide range of strategies to comprehend, interpret, evaluate, and appreciate texts. Draw on prior experience, interactions with other readers and writers, knowledge of word meaning and of other texts, word identification strategies, and understanding of textual features (e.g., sound-letter correspondence, sentence structure, context, graphics).

Objective

Students will create a sequential, visual representation of the major events in a story.

Materials

tag board
markers

Drawing a storyboard is a reading strategy that encourages students to visualize a story. It challenges them to recall the sequence of events, an important comprehension skill. Use this activity with a story from a basal reader or other assigned reading.

1. Make storyboard strips by cutting sheets of tag board in half lengthwise. Give two long half-sheets to each student. Direct students to fold each strip in half twice. Each strip will have four sections. Have students tape the two strips together to make one long strip of eight sections. (Some students may need more than eight sections to complete their storyboard, so have extra tag board strips on hand. However, limit students to no more than ten sections to encourage them to remain focused on major events.)

2. Instruct students to write the book title and author in the first section. This will be the only section that includes words.

3. Explain that a storyboard is sometimes used by book illustrators and filmmakers to show the main events of a story. Events are shown in the order in which they happen. Instruct students to plan each section of the storyboard to show one important event that moves the story along. Have students make a list of their story events before they begin to draw.

4. After students have illustrated their storyboards, have them share their completed artwork with the class. Fold the strips accordion-style to stand up for display on top of bookcases, windowsills, and tables. Storyboards create great displays for an open house!

Ideas for More Differentiation

As you read aloud to students from a favorite book, encourage them to close their eyes and create mental pictures. Select passages with vivid depictions or sensory descriptions that will help students imagine color, taste, smell, sound, and touch. Make text selections short but powerful. Invite students to share descriptive passages they encounter in their reading, as well.

The Cricket in Times Square

Standard

Apply a wide range of strategies to comprehend, interpret, evaluate, and appreciate texts. Draw on prior experience, interactions with other readers and writers, knowledge of word meaning and of other texts, word identification strategies, and understanding of textual features (e.g., sound-letter correspondence, sentence structure, context, graphics).

Objective

Students will use a cubing technique to select a method to respond to literature.

Materials

Cricket Questions Cube reproducible
multiple copies of *The Cricket in Times Square* by George Selden
heavy paper
tape or glue
scissors

Give students the opportunity to use and share what they have learned as they read the classic story *The Cricket in Times Square* by George Selden. Cubing activities provide students with opportunities for success using problem-solving and thinking skills.

1. In this variation on a cubing activity, students will toss a cube to select a method of responding to what they have read. Choose a focus chapter, or have students choose a chapter on their own.

2. Copy the **Cricket Questions Cube reproducible (page 73)** onto heavy paper, ▶ and cut it out. Fold the squares to form a cube. Tape or glue the

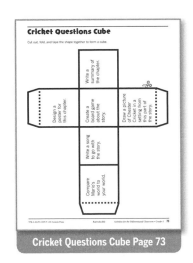

Cricket Questions Cube Page 73

tabs in place. Make as many cubes as needed to accommodate your class. Have each student or group of students roll the cube to choose an activity to complete.

- **Write** a summary of the chapter.

- **Draw** a picture of Chester Cricket in a setting from this part of the story.

- **Create** a board game about the story.

- **Design** a poster for this chapter.

- **Write** a song to go with the story.

- **Compare** Mario's world to your world.

3. This cubing activity accommodates a variety of learning styles. Use it repeatedly with other chapters from the book. Establish a rule that students must roll the cube until they get a different prompt from the previous roll.

Ideas for More Differentiation

Create activity lists that address specific learning styles. Write and number each idea on a chart. Have students roll a die. The number on the die corresponds to a numbered activity on the list.

Make a list of movement activities for bodily/kinesthetic learners:

1. Create a cricket dance.

2. Role-play a scene from the chapter.

3. Make a model of the newsstand or another place in the story.

4. Create a party for Chester and his friends.

5. Act out a scene that takes place after the end of the story.

6. Create an outdoor game based on the story.

Make a list of drawing/design activities for visual/spatial learners:

1. Design a cover for the book.

2. Make a collage about the story.

3. Create a banner for the newsstand.

4. Design a newspaper ad for Chester's concert.

5. Draw a picture or make a model of Grand Central Station.

6. Create a travel poster for New York or Chinatown.

Cricket Questions Cube

Cut out, fold, and tape the shape together to form a cube.

Write a summary of the chapter.

Design a poster for this chapter.

Create a board game about the story.

Draw a picture of Chester Cricket in a setting from this part of the story.

Write a song to go with the story.

Compare Mario's world to your world.

What's the Word?

Standard

Apply a wide range of strategies to comprehend, interpret, evaluate, and appreciate texts. Draw on prior experience, interactions with other readers and writers, knowledge of word meaning and of other texts, word identification strategies, and understanding of textual features (e.g., sound-letter correspondence, sentence structure, context, graphics).

Objective

Students will match vocabulary words with definitions.

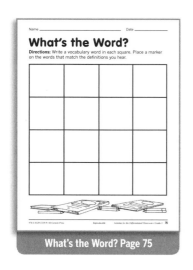

What's the Word? Page 75

Materials

What's the Word? reproducible
game board markers

Play a simple Bingo-like game to help students recall word meanings. Rehearsal activities such as this one are fun to play, and they build reading vocabulary and word identification skills. Both English language learners and English speakers can develop word skills with this game.

1. Give students a copy of the **What's the Word? reproducible (page 75)**. Write 16 vocabulary words on the board. Have students write each word in a square on their game board. Tell them to write the words in random order so their game board will be different from everyone else's. Give each student a handful of game markers.

2. Define a word, and challenge students to find that word on their game board and place a marker on it. When students have covered four words in a row (horizontally, vertically, or diagonally), they call out: *What's the word!* As you define words, keep a list of the words you use. When a students wins, have him or her read their words aloud so you can check for accuracy.

3. Have students clear their cards and begin the game again. Invite them to exchange cards if they like.

Name _____ Date _____

What's the Word?

Directions: Write a vocabulary word in each square. Place a marker on the words that match the definitions you hear.

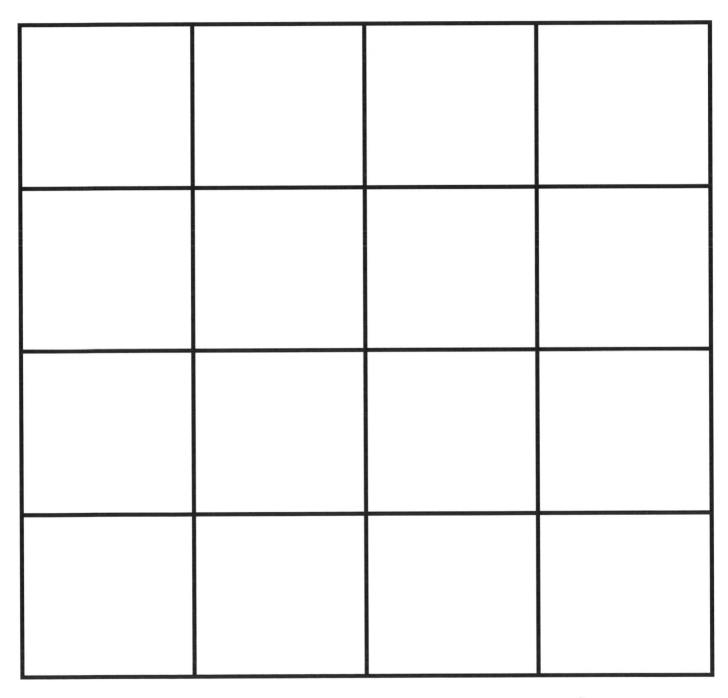

Table of Contents

Standard

Apply a wide range of strategies to comprehend, interpret, evaluate, and appreciate texts. Draw on prior experience, interactions with other readers and writers, knowledge of word meaning and of other texts, word identification strategies, and understanding of textual features (e.g., sound-letter correspondence, sentence structure, context, graphics).

Objective

Students will ask and answer questions about a table of contents from a book.

Materials

books with different kinds of tables of contents
chart paper
markers

This rotation activity invites students to study a table of contents in order to answer questions created by other students. It also requires them to create their own questions. Students should carefully consider what they read in order to complete the activities. The questions they ask and answer will lead to a deeper understanding of the information found in a table of contents.

1. Establish five or six centers around the room. At each center, place a book with a table of contents, a sheet of chart paper, and a marker.

2. Divide the class into small groups. Have each group start at one center and rotate to the other centers.

3. Instruct each group to read the book's table of contents and create a question that can be answered using on the information they find there. The group's recorder writes the question on the chart paper. Give students the following examples of the types of questions they might ask:

    • *How many chapters are in the book?*

    • *What will you find on page 15?*

    • *What is the title of the poem in this book?*

- *What is the main topic of the book?*

- *Which two chapters would you read to find the differences between birds and mammals?*

- *Who is the author of the short story "One Sun"?*

4. After students have written a question at the first center, give a signal for all the groups to rotate to the next center. At the second center, challenge students to first answer the question the previous group has written. Then invite them to compose a question of their own for the next group to answer. When students have had time to complete both tasks, give the signal again. Have groups rotate to the third center. Continue until each group has visited every center.

5. When students have completed their tasks at all the centers, post the charts around the classroom. Have the groups share some of the questions and answers on their charts. Students will be interested to see how others answered the questions they composed.

Ideas for More Differentiation

Encourage students to exercise their linguistic skills by developing a table of contents for an imaginary book. Provide titles of real or invented nonfiction books on slips of paper. Have students work in pairs to choose a slip and create a table of contents for that book title. They will have to research the topic using encyclopedias and other resources to decide what subtopics to include and how to organize their table of contents. Invite students to refer to other tables of contents and include all the necessary elements, such as chapter titles and page numbers.

Wiki Tiki Words

Standard
Apply a wide range of strategies to comprehend, interpret, evaluate, and appreciate texts. Draw on prior experience, interactions with other readers and writers, knowledge of word meaning and of other texts, word identification strategies, and understanding of textual features (e.g., sound-letter correspondence, sentence structure, context, graphics).

Objective
Students will provide missing words in a listening game.

Materials
read-aloud book

This entertaining game encourages students to tune in and develop their attention spans. It is a simple and quick way to provide a comprehension challenge, requiring listeners to predict what comes next. Even the best listeners can be stumped, which makes the game even more fun for all!

1. Choose a story, chapter, or short selection or passage to read aloud to the class.

2. Divide the class into two teams. Teams can remain in their seats or stand in two lines.

3. Explain that you will read the story aloud but pause at certain points before finishing a sentence. When students hear you say: *Wiki Tiki Word*, invite them to suggest the next word in the sentence.

4. Have teams alternate guessing. If a player on Team A says an incorrect word, give the player on Team B a turn. If the player on Team A says a correct word, give the player on Team B first chance on the next word. Teams score one point for each correct Wiki Tiki Word. The team with the most points at the end of the story is the Wiki Tiki winner!

Biography Scrapbook

Strategy
Topic-related project

Standard
Use spoken, written, and visual language to accomplish a purpose (e.g., for learning, enjoyment, persuasion, and the exchange of information).

Objective
Students will read a biography and create a scrapbook page that reflects the life of the subject.

Materials
variety of biographies
construction paper
magazines
art supplies

Encourage students to read biographies and then create a project that illustrates what they learned about the life of their subject. In this "crafty" book report, students make a scrapbook page to show important people, places, and events in the life of their subject.

1. Assign each student a biography to read. Encourage students to think visually about the life of the subject. Ask them to step into the shoes of that person and create a page from a scrapbook that he or she might have kept.

2. Invite the class to brainstorm some ideas about the types of things people save in a scrapbook. If you have a scrapbook, consider sharing it with the class. Photos, newspaper clippings, small mementos, menus, ticket stubs, postcards, autographs, programs from plays or concerts, business cards, greeting cards, invitations, and announcements are some of the items people save in scrapbooks.

3. As an example, discuss a scrapbook page that could be created for the great Russian ballerina Anna Pavlova. It might include a photo of a swan, a newspaper clipping about her wildly popular ballet performance in a Mexican bullring, a recipe for a Pavlova (a dessert named for her), a white feather from her swan costume, postcards from her travels in Australia and the United States, a thank-you note from one of her students, a train or boat ticket, and a program from one of her performances.

4. Give each student a large sheet of construction paper to create a scrapbook page. Invite students to use their imagination to craft mementos using a variety of art supplies, including colored paper, crayons or markers, magazine pictures, various fonts or graphics, stickers, fabric scraps, scissors, and glue.

5. Display the finished projects on a bulletin board titled *Scrapbook Pages from History.* When it's time to take down the display, bind the pages into a keepsake scrapbook for the classroom library.

Ideas for More Differentiation

Tap into students' interests and multiple intelligences by providing project alternatives for biography book reports.

- Paint a portrait. Make your subject look as you think he or she would want to be remembered. (visual/spatial learners)

- Create a dance. Illustrate an event or something important in the life of your subject. (bodily/kinesthetic learners)

- Write a short play. Create a scene from the person's life using two or three actors. (bodily/kinesthetic learners)

- Become a pet. Imagine you are the person's pet attending an important event. Write what your owner does, and tell what you think about it. (verbal/linguistic and naturalist learners)

Team Sentences

Standard

Apply knowledge of language structure, language conventions (e.g., spelling and punctuation), media techniques, figurative language, and genre to create, critique, and discuss print and nonprint texts.

Strategies
Rehearsal

Game

Objective

Students will work in teams to write complete, correct sentences.

In this exciting relay game, students collaborate with their team members to write a complete sentence using correct spelling and punctuation. The first team to do so earns a point. This task gets students up on their feet and requires everyone to think ahead.

1. Divide the class into four teams. Have each team line up at a distance from the board. Assign each team a place to write.

2. Explain to students that you will say one word, such as *my, we,* or *they*. The first player on each team will go to the board as quickly as possible, write the word you said, and add a word before or after it as the first step to building a complete sentence. The players then go back to their teams and hand the marker or chalk to the next player in line.

3. The next player adds a word to the sentence, and so on, until the last player on the team takes a turn. Though they must work quickly, players should do their best to use readable writing and correct spelling. Each player must be careful not to finish the sentence before the last student takes a turn.

4. The last student on each team adds the final word to complete the sentence. This player also has the important job of proofreading and correcting what has been written and adding capitalization and punctuation to finish the sentence. The first team whose sentence is complete and correct scores a point. Erase the board and begin with a new word.

Liven Up Handwriting Practice

Standard
Adjust use of spoken, written, and visual language (e.g., conventions, style, vocabulary) to communicate effectively with a variety of audiences and for different purposes.

Objective
Students will use alternative methods to improve handwriting skills.

Materials
craft sticks
clean, empty soup can or pencil cup

Use this focus activity to build on students' enthusiasm for learning cursive writing. These activities help bodily/kinesthetic learners focus on important aspects of the new letters they are learning. Handwriting practice that involves large muscle movement encourages fine muscle coordination and establishes muscle memory for cursive letters.

- Invite students to write cursive letters in the air using different body parts, such as hands, elbows, nose, chin, and knees. Write each student's name on a craft stick, and place the sticks in a soup can or pencil cup. Select a craft stick. Ask that student to choose a body part for the class to use to write a cursive letter in the air.

- Ask students to write a "letter of the day" on the floor with their foot. Challenge them to repeat the activity using their non-dominant foot.

- Have students "ice skate" in a large, open space. Invite them to write a letter the way a figure skater makes a figure eight. Focus on particular groups of letters such as those beginning with loops. Do this with letters that students find particularly challenging.

- Focus on correct writing posture. Compare the importance of correct body position when writing to correct body position when playing baseball or golf. The body needs to be in the correct position to perform at its best. Chair placement, elbow position, paper slant, hand and head positions, and foot placement help students focus on performance.

Ideas for More Differentiation
Play favorite classical music selections as students practice handwriting. Music speaks to both sides of the brain and helps focus attention.

Physical Education, Art, and Music

Pick It Up!

Objective

Students will follow nonverbal prompts to practice movement skills.

Materials

Pick It Up! Challenge Cards reproducibles
heavy paper
scissors

Challenge students to use their linguistic skills for reading as well as for following auditory directions. In this game, students read a challenge card and do the activity until it's time to change to a different one. This stimulates language development, thinking, and creativity.

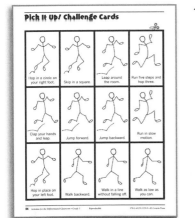

Pick It Up! Challenge Cards Page 84–85

1. Copy the **Pick It Up! Challenge Cards reproducibles (pages 84–85)** on heavy paper, and cut out the cards. Laminate the cards for greater durability. Prepare twice as many cards as there will be students playing.

2. Scatter the challenge cards facedown on the floor. At your signal, invite students to move freely around the room. When you call out: *Pick it up!* have each player pick up a challenge card.

3. Have students read their card, place it back on the floor, and then perform the movement printed on the card. Have students continue moving until you give another command. You can tell students to pick up another challenge card or do a specific movement, such as skipping to the other side of the room.

Ideas for More Differentiation

Modify this activity so it is strictly nonverbal. Form relay teams. Scatter the challenge cards on the floor on the opposite side of the room. One team member at a time runs across the room, picks up a card, reads it, and performs the movement on the return trip.

Pick It Up! Challenge Cards

Hop in a circle on your right foot.

Skip in a square.

Leap around the room.

Run five steps and hop three.

Clap your hands and leap.

Jump forward.

Jump backward.

Run in slow motion.

Hop in place on your left foot.

Walk backward.

Walk in a line without falling off.

Walk as low as you can.

Pick It Up! Challenge Cards

Skip in a
giant circle.

Jump forward and
then backward.

Skip backward.

Hop sideways
on one foot.

Run in place.

Walk as fast as
you can.

Hop with your
arms folded.

Jump left and
then right.

Walk as if you
are tired.

Jump high
and twist.

Skip in a zigzag.

Run four steps
and touch
the floor.

Pick It Up! Challenge Cards

Gallop like
a horse.

Slide to
your right.

Run on your toes.

Jump back and
forth over a line.

Bend over while
you walk.

Raise your knees
high while
you run.

Slide away from
your spot
and slide back.

Move like an
ice skater.

Hop three times on
one foot and three
times on the other.

Run and splash
through "puddles."

Jiggle while
you walk.

Jump, clap, jump,
clap, jump, clap!

Water Dances

Objective
Students will interpret water in movement and create a dance.

Strategy
Exhibition

Materials
Water Dances reproducible
pictures of water in various forms
heavy paper
drum

Inspire students to think about water in its many forms and create movements that expand on water's characteristics. Have them select two water movements and create a movement sequence that follows a pattern. This activity engages students' imagination, physical energy, and personal expression.

1. Display pictures from magazines and books of water in various forms, such as ocean waves, a fountain spray, a geyser, a rainstorm, ice floes, falling snowflakes, and a swimming pool. Invite students to think about how the water in each picture moves. Have them interpret this movement with their bodies. Encourage them to exaggerate their gestures.

2. Copy the **Water Dances reproducible (page 88)** on heavy paper, and cut apart the pictures of various forms of water in motion. Make enough copies so each student gets two pictures. Invite students to create movements that reflect their two pictures.

3. Explain that students will be creating a dance about water using the movements they invented for their pictures. Dances often follow a pattern. The pattern for their dance will be ABA. This means they choose one picture to be A and one picture to be B. They will perform their movements in that order—A, B, and then A again.

4. Take students to a wide, open area. Play a steady drumbeat and call out *A!* Continue for playing the drum for several beats before calling out *B* and for several more before calling *A* again. Give students several opportunities to perform their dances in this way.

5. Collect and redistribute the picture cards so students can create a different dance. At another time, vary the pattern. For example, invite students to create a dance with an ABBA or ABAB pattern.

▶
Water Dances Page 88

Water Dances

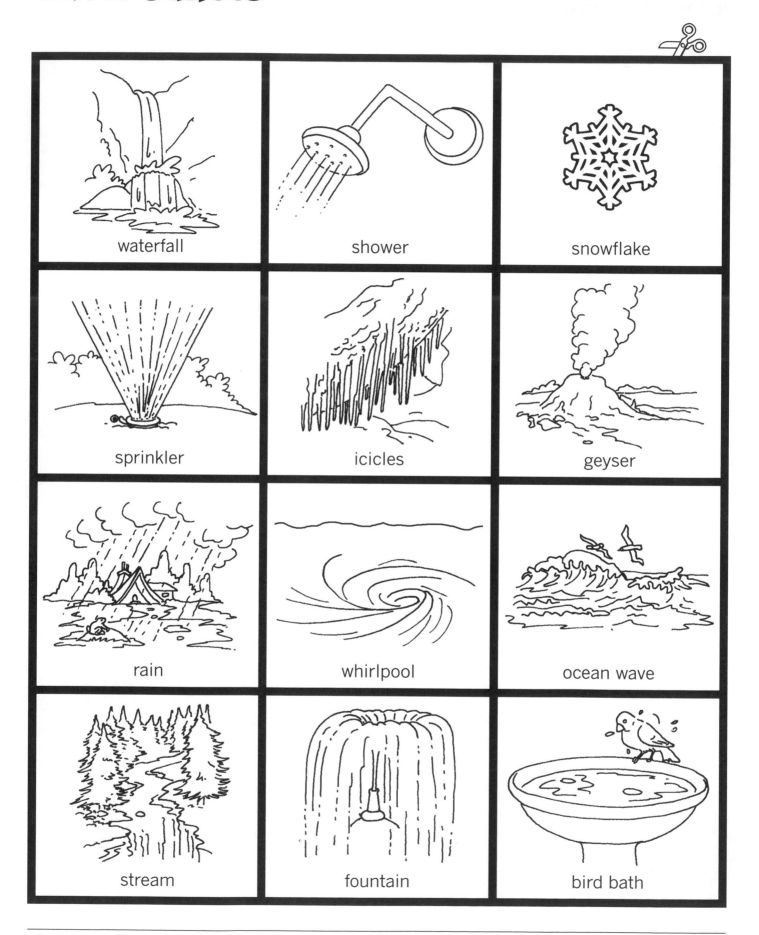

waterfall	shower	snowflake
sprinkler	icicles	geyser
rain	whirlpool	ocean wave
stream	fountain	bird bath

Starfish in the Sea

Objective
Students will exercise to increase cardiovascular fitness.

Materials
Starfish in the Sea reproducible
masking tape

In this game, "starfish" wash up on the shore and go back into the ocean. Some students are ocean waves and others are surfers. The surfers pick up the starfish and dive back into the water with them. But the ocean waves keep bringing more to shore. Who will win? It doesn't matter, because everyone gets a good workout!

1. Make several copies of the **Starfish in the Sea reproducible (page 90)**. Cut ▶ out the cards so you have plenty of starfish. Using masking tape, make a line down the center of a large, open area. Spread the starfish all over the area, placing an equal number of starfish on both sides of the line.

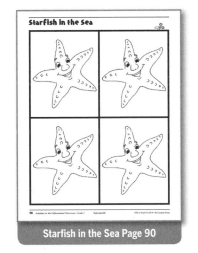

Starfish in the Sea Page 90

2. Divide students into two equal groups. One group will be ocean waves, and the other group will be surfers. Assign each group to one side of the line. At your signal, invite the ocean waves to move the starfish from their side of the line (ocean) to the other side of the line (shore). At the same time, invite the surfers to move the starfish from their side of the line (shore) to the other side of the line (ocean). Each player may pick up only two starfish at one time. Play for about a minute before allowing students to rest and catch their breath.

3. When students are ready, begin another round. In subsequent rounds, vary the type of movement. Instead of running to move starfish, invite students to hop, skip, jump, or walk like a crab.

4. Collect all the starfish, and save them for another time. Make a game of collecting them by forming relay teams. At your signal, have team members take turns running to pick up a starfish and take it back to their team's pile (they may only grab one starfish at a time). When all starfish are collected, the team with the most starfish wins.

Starfish in the Sea

Reproducible 978-1-4129-5339-9 • © Corwin Press

Visiting Grandma Moses

Objective
Students will describe Grandma Moses' art style and subject matter.

Materials
Visiting Grandma Moses reproducible
The Grandma Moses Night Before Christmas Poem by Clement C. Moore
The Year with Grandma Moses by W. Nikola-Lisa
dark blue construction paper
chalks or pastels

Aesthetic perception involves students' making choices rather than giving correct answers. Learning to see a painting and think about it from a new perspective helps students develop an appreciation for art that is all around them.

Grandma Moses was an American folk artist. She began painting when she was in her seventies and never had an art lesson. She turned to painting when arthritis made it hard for her to embroider. Most of her paintings depict realistic scenes of life in the country as she remembered it growing up in the 1880s. Her style was simple, lively, and colorful.

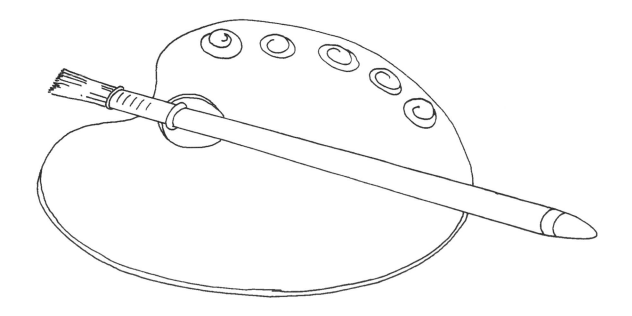

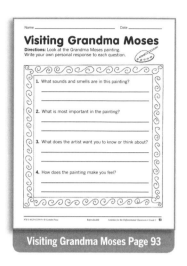

1. Share with students some picture books illustrated with Grandma Moses' paintings. You might also find prints of her works in reference books and on the Internet.

2. Give students a copy of the **Visiting Grandma Moses reproducible (page 93)**. Choose a painting from one of the picture books, and ask students to answer the questions on the reproducible with this painting in mind. Discuss their answers and insights. Emphasize that all responses are valid and that there is not one correct answer to any of the questions.

3. Give each student a sheet of dark blue construction paper to use as a background. Invite students to use chalk to create an outdoor scene in a style Grandma Moses might have used. For example, Grandma Moses painted scenes that were familiar to her. Invite students to draw a busy scene they are familiar with, such as a school playground, their neighborhood street, or a shopping center. Invite them to show people going about their lives. Have students add themselves participating in a favorite activity to the picture.

4. Display students' artwork in a classroom art gallery. Invite students to title their pictures in a way that describes the scenes.

Ideas for More Differentiation

Bodily/kinesthetic learners can create a *tableau vivant* of a favorite Grandma Moses painting. A *tableau vivant* is a scene with costumed actors who remain silent and motionless as if in a picture. Have a group of students work together to paint a backdrop on butcher paper and make simple props from boxes. Use simple clothing, such as hats and scarves, for costumes. Encourage students to share their *tableau vivant* with another class, displaying the Grandma Moses inspiration picture alongside their portrayal.

Visiting Grandma Moses

Directions: Look at the Grandma Moses painting.
Write your own personal response to each question.

1. What sounds and smells are in this painting?

_____

_____

2. What is most important in the painting?

_____

_____

3. What does the artist want you to know or think about?

_____

_____

4. How does the painting make you feel?

_____

_____

The Outrageous Onomatopoeia Orchestra

Strategy
Multiple intelligences

Objective
Students will create a musical variation using onomatopoeic words.

Materials
chart paper

Students delight in word play. Word play and music seem to naturally fit together. Invite students to explore rhythm and voice to create an orchestra of sounds.

1. Begin by brainstorming onomatopoeic words—words that imitate sounds of the objects they refer to. Make a chart of the words students suggest. Your list may include *buzz, hiss, slurp, tick-tock, woof, z-z-zip, screech, eek, squeak, oompah, thrum, honk, pop, tinkle,* and *gong.*

2. Divide the class into small groups of five or six. Explain that each group will create an onomatopoeia orchestra. Instead of playing instruments, they will say words. Have each group member choose a different word to say.

3. Encourage students to develop their own rhythm and practice saying their word in that rhythm. Some rhythms may be short and staccato; some may be long and drawn out; some may emphasize the first beat; and some may emphasize the final beat. Encourage variety and creativity.

4. Once students have established their own rhythm and practiced their words, they are ready to assemble their orchestra. Direct the first student to begin by saying his or her word in the rhythm practiced. Have the second student add his or her word. Continue until all students in the orchestra are simultaneously chanting their onomatopoeic words. After rehearsing, invite students to perform for the class.

    978-1-4129-5339-9

Lullabies

Objective

Students will explore qualities of familiar lullabies and bedtime stories.

Strategy
Multiple intelligences

Materials

Grandfather Twilight by Barbara Berger
recording of "Clair de Lune" by Claude Debussy
recordings of lullabies

Help students recognize and appreciate that music can provide an island of quiet in a busy world. Help them slow down during a busy day by exposing them to the quiet beauty and tender music of lullabies.

1. Introduce students to the calm and relaxing music of Debussy's "Clair de Lune." As you play a recording of this composition, read aloud the gentle story of *Grandfather Twilight* by Barbara Berger. The glowing pictures and poetic story will enchant students and bring them to a peaceful hush. Grandfather Twilight magically spreads twilight each evening with a glowing pearl he carries to the edge of sea where it becomes the moon.

2. Ask students if they can remember a lullaby that was sung to them when they were a baby. Invite them to bring in recordings of favorite lullabies to share with the class. Some students might volunteer to teach the class a lullaby from their family's tradition or a lullaby in another language.

3. Invite students to bring in favorite bedtime stories as well. Share some picture book classics such as *Goodnight Moon* by Margaret Wise Brown.

References

Armstrong, T. (2000). *Multiple intelligences in the classroom.* Alexandria, VA: Association for Supervision and Curriculum Development.

Berger, M., & Berger, G. (2005). *Solar system.* New York, NY : Scholastic, Inc.

Burns, S. (2000). Moses, Grandma. In *World book encyclopedia* (Vol. 13, p. 830). Chicago, IL: World Book, Inc.

Campbell, D. (2000). *The Mozart effect for children.* New York, NY: William Morrow.

Chapman, C., & King, R. (2003). *Differentiated instructional strategies for reading in the content areas.* Thousand Oaks, CA: Corwin Press, Inc.

Dauben, J. W. (2000). Science. In *World book encyclopedia* (Vol. 17, pp. 191–204). Chicago, IL: World Book, Inc.

Dunn, M. G. (Ed.). (1989). *Exploring your world.* Washington, D.C.: National Geographic Society.

Gregory, G. H., & Chapman, C. (2002). *Differentiated instructional strategies: One size doesn't fit all, second edition.* Thousand Oaks, CA: Corwin Press.

Hurwitz, A., Goddard, A., & Epstein, D. T. (1975). *Number games to improve your child's arithmetic.* New York, NY: Funk and Wagnalls.

Lewis, J. J. (n.d.) *About women's history.* Retrieved November 6, 2006, from http://womenshistory.about.com/library/bio/blbio_list_science.htm.

Mandell, M. (1975). *Games to learn by.* New York, NY: Sterling Publishing Co.

Murden, J. (1993). *Stars and planets.* New York, NY: Kingfisher.

National Council for the Social Studies. (2002). *Expectations of excellence: Curriculum standards for social studies.* Silver Spring, MD: National Council for the Social Studies (NCSS).

National Council of Teachers of English and International Reading Association. (1996). *Standards for the English language arts.* Urbana, IL: National Council of Teachers of English (NCTE).

National Council of Teachers of Mathematics. (2005). *Principles and standards for school mathematics.* Reston, VA: National Council of Teachers of Mathematics (NCTM).

National Research Council. (2005). *National science education standards.* Washington, D.C.: National Academy Press.

Seabrooke, K. (Ed.). (2006). *The world almanac for kids 2006.* New York, NY: World Almanac Books.

Sobel, S. (2001). *The U.S. Constitution and you.* Hauppage, NY: Barron's Educational Series, Inc.